Morris Minor

Morris Minor

A collector's guide
by Guy Saddlestone

MOTOR RACING PUBLICATIONS LTD
Unit 6, The Pilton Estate, 46 Pitlake, Croydon CR0 3RY, England

First published 1997

British Library Cataloguing in Publication Data

Saddlestone, Guy
   Morris Minor : a collector's guide
   1. Morris Minor automobile – Collectors and collecting
   I. Title
   629.2'222

ISBN 1-899870-17-2

Printed in Great Britain by
The Amadeus Press Ltd
Huddersfield, West Yorkshire

Contents

Introduction and acknowledgements

So why shouldn't I continue to drive a 30-year-old car which costs me next to nothing to maintain, provides unfailing reliability, and gets me where I'm going as quickly and as comfortably as I could wish for? A lot of my friends have tried to provide answers to that question, but none of them have yet been convincing. Minors, in my opinion, were made to be used, and the genius of their design is that they can still be used, half a century after the first examples took to the roads.

After I'd been running Minors for many years, it occurred to me to find out exactly what lay behind this remarkable piece of machinery, and it was then that I started looking into the history of the design. What I found delighted me, and I've tried to convey some of that delight in discovery through the pages of this book. I hope it gives you as much pleasure to read as it gave me to write.

A lot of people provided both inspiration and information for this book. My thanks go to all of them. In particular, I'd like to thank Joe Swords at *Minor Monthly* – the only British magazine devoted exclusively to the marque – for his assistance. Many of the pictures between these covers come from the archives of that magazine and from the cameras of Tony Aston, Jon Betts and Robert Hawkins.

April 1997   Guy Saddlestone

CHAPTER 1

In the beginning

Alec Issigonis and the Mosquito

You can put the whole of the concept and design of the postwar Morris Minor down to the engineering genius of one man, and that man was Alec Issigonis. Issigonis, who was also responsible for the revolutionary BMC Mini a decade later, was of Greek origin but had come to Britain in 1922 with his parents to escape from the Turkish invasion of his native Smyrna. He studied engineering in London, found a job with a small motor industry components supplier, and was quickly talent-spotted by the chief engineer of the Rootes Group. At Rootes, he specialized in suspension design, but then he was once again talent-spotted, this time by the chief engineer of Morris. So during 1936, Issigonis moved to Morris' Cowley headquarters, where he was put to work on the suspension of the forthcoming Series M Ten, which was to be the company's first unitary-construction car.

The Series M Ten entered production in 1938, but without the new front suspension and rack-and-pinion steering which Issigonis had designed for it. Both were considered insufficiently developed at the time, although Issigonis did continue to work on them and had them ready for a new small MG saloon which was scheduled to enter production as a 1940 model. The outbreak of war in September 1939 prevented that car from going into production, however, and so Issigonis was frustrated once again. It would be 1947 before his designs would reach the showrooms, when the prewar MG saloon finally did go into production as the Y-type.

Nevertheless, Alec Issigonis was the sort of good man you can't keep down. As early as 1941, while engaged on war work for what was now called the Nuffield Organisation (named after Lord Nuffield, born William Morris), he supplemented his thinking about armoured car and tank design with schemes for a new car. This time, Issigonis was not content with suspension design alone. Instead, he devoted his engineering talent to the design of a complete car – and the remarkable thing about it was that this car was not the sum total of a collection of existing components but rather a homogeneous entity where each part was designed specifically to complement the next.

Issigonis never appears to have been in any doubt about what he wanted, and the surviving early sketches for the car which eventually became the Morris Minor show an extraordinarily close resemblance to the production model. Right at the heart of Issigonis' thinking was the firm belief that a car should be designed to carry the maximum possible payload of passengers and luggage within the minimum possible space. In other words, the mechanical elements should be constructed and arranged so that they occupied as little space as possible within the overall package. As Issigonis had no interest in ostentation and styling, he was inevitably drawn towards designing a small car.

Meanwhile, Miles Thomas had been appointed as the new Vice-Chairman and Managing Director of the Nuffield Organisation. Thomas was a far-sighted individual and, in contrast to Lord Nuffield, who remained Chairman, he was receptive to new ideas. It was his view – though hardly an

The original Morris Minor was introduced in 1928 to cash in on the market which the Austin Seven had opened up. It was replaced in 1931 by a new Minor – seen here – which featured a side-valve engine instead of the original's ohc type. The car lasted until 1934, but there was then no Morris Minor until Issigonis' design was announced in 1948, its place in the range being occupied by successive versions of the Morris Eight.

original one – that Nuffield would need a small car when the war was over, as small cars offered the best chances of high-volume production and the high profits which came with that. He discussed his views with A V (Vic) Oak, who was then the chief engineer at Cowley; Oak, of course, knew of Alec Issigonis' designs for a small car; and in due course the three men got together to talk over ideas. With this high-level encouragement, Issigonis was allowed to continue working on his designs for a small car alongside the war work he was doing for Nuffield.

In fact, Issigonis was given quite exceptional treatment. He was taken out of the main Drawing Office at Morris' Cowley works and was given his own self-contained development shop in a corner of the factory. Vic Oak allocated to him a pair of draughtsmen whose job it was to turn his ideas into drawings from which components could be made, and more or less left the three of them to get on with the job. It was Jack Daniels who drew up the running gear for the new car, while Reg Job became the body

draughtsman. Issigonis remained the visionary, but the small team gelled extremely well and the car which resulted was all the better for it.

By 1942, Issigonis had a ½th-scale wooden model of the car he wanted, and from this he had drawings taken. These drawings were scaled-up, and from them was built the first hand-made running prototype. This came together slowly during 1943, its bodyshell being assembled in the experimental bodyshop at Cowley, and by December 1 that year the completed car was ready for the road. It bore the identifying number EX/SX/86 (experimental, 6hp, fleet number 86) and was known as a Morris Mosquito.

No-one now remembers for certain who gave it that name, but the idea may well have come from Miles Thomas. As a former fighter pilot, he would have taken a keen interest in the exploits of the contemporary De Havilland Mosquito fighter-bomber and the name would have been on his mind. The fact that mosquitoes are insects and therefore small was also very appropriate

The prototype Morris Mosquito, which was built in 1943, seen wearing one of several radiator grilles which were tried during the course of the car's development into the Minor. The familiar shape is already evident as proof that Alec Issigonis got it right first time.

because Issigonis' new car was itself small.

It was inevitable that the Mosquito should have had a unitary bodyshell, if only because Morris had already embarked on unitary construction with the 1938 Series M 10hp model. The smaller Series E 8hp introduced at the same time had a compromise semi-unitary construction. Nevertheless, the Mosquito's structure was an interesting one, with the floorpan bordered by box-section sill members and braced longitudinally by box-section rails which extended forwards to act as supports for the engine and front suspension. To that were welded body side members and roof bracing, and the outer skin panels and roof were then dropped into place over this inner framework.

While this method of construction was still new, it was not particularly innovative. The Mosquito's appearance was startlingly different from anything which had ever come from Nuffield before, though. Alec Issigonis never claimed to be a stylist, and for him the overriding principle was that form followed function. Even so, the shape which was

carried through almost unaltered to the production Minor was an important element of the car's character, and it is interesting to see what might have influenced Issigonis' thinking. It certainly wasn't existing Nuffield designs: the Morris, Wolseley, Riley and MG models in production when the war broke out were all fairly traditional in their use of upright radiators and separate running-boards, and the Mosquito had neither of these features.

Quite probably, Issigonis had been influenced by the latest styling from America (where the war did not disrupt production until 1942), and in particular the 1941 Packard Clipper. He may also have absorbed some ideas from the 1936 Fiat 500, the leading small car of the time, and for the idea of concealing the headlamps behind the radiator grille he may have been influenced by Peugeot designs of the Thirties. For the oval grille itself, however, it is difficult to find a precedent – and it is perhaps significant that this was the one styling feature with which Issigonis tinkered on several occasions during the prototype stage.

Issigonis had originally made his name at Rootes and at

9

Cowley as a suspension engineer, and so it was no surprise that the Mosquito incorporated some interesting ideas in this area. Like many other engineers of his generation, Issigonis had been greatly impressed by the torsion-bar suspension of the 1934 Citroën *Traction Avant*, and he incorporated similar design principles into the Mosquito. He had also met and admired Maurice Olley, the American suspension engineer who had designed the independent front suspension introduced on General Motors models in 1933, while Olley was working with Vauxhall in Britain. So the Mosquito had independent front suspension with torsion-bar springs, a design which gave the best possible handling and roadholding and also minimized the space taken up by the suspension.

This wish to save space – remember that Issigonis believed space was best utilized for the passengers and their luggage – was also behind the Mosquito's use of rack-and-pinion steering. Put simply, this type of steering took up much less space than more conventional types, and Issigonis also liked it for its engineering simplicity. The fact that it brought marked improvements in handling and steering control was simply an added bonus.

It was space once again which had persuaded Issigonis to design a flat-four engine for the Mosquito. As the car was to be small, the choice of a four-cylinder engine was automatic: engines with fewer cylinders brought balance and refinement problems, and engines with more cylinders brought additional size, expense and engineering complication. However, the traditional in-line four-cylinder engine was both tall and long. Issigonis reasoned that by having the cylinders in opposed pairs he could almost halve the length of the engine, and that by having them laid out horizontally he could reduce the height by an even bigger amount. The short, wide engine which resulted would also have benefits for the car's handling by concentrating weight low down in its nose and thus lowering its centre of gravity. By allowing for alternative cylinder barrel sizes, it would be possible to produce an 800cc engine to fit into the cheap 6hp taxation class in Britain, and a larger 1,100cc variant to suit overseas markets where power was more important.

Was it space considerations again which persuaded Issigonis to use a three-speed gearbox with a column-mounted change mechanism? The logic behind the design suggests it was. There was no three-speed car gearbox in production anywhere in the Nuffield Organisation, but a three-speed gearbox would inevitably have been smaller (as well as simpler in engineering terms) than a conventional four-speed type. Similarly, Issigonis wanted his new car to have a bench front seat with enough room for three people – which would have been impossible with a floor-mounted gearchange lever. So the lever had to go onto the column, which was where some American and European makers had already begun to locate their gearchanges.

Last but not least, most cars of the late Thirties had 16-inch or 17-inch wheels, but Issigonis' Mosquito had tiny 14-inch ones. The designer himself always maintained that the main reason for this was appearance and that bigger wheels would have unbalanced the styling. However, it is also true that the small wheels served his primary interest of minimizing the space taken up by the car's running gear. Larger wheels would have required larger wheelarches which in turn would have eaten into the space available for the passenger compartment and the boot. Using these small wheels was a more revolutionary step than it may appear at first sight, too. At the time 14-inch wheels and tyres simply weren't available in Britain, and when the Morris Minor went into production in 1948, Dunlop had to be persuaded to manufacture both wheels and tyres specially for the car.

For 1943, then, the Mosquito was an astonishingly advanced piece of design, especially for a car maker as conventional as Morris. However, there was no chance that it could go into production yet. Britain was still at war and the car makers were still devoting their efforts to building or repairing trucks, aeroplanes and tanks. Car production had stopped in 1940 and would not resume until the Government permitted it in 1945. So during 1944, 1945 and the first part of 1946, Alec Issigonis had to be content with refining and perfecting his design. The single prototype Mosquito was modified several times, was used to try out different suspension systems which included a torsion-bar independent rear suspension, and was painted grey over its original black. Yet no further prototypes were made until September 1946, by which time Morris had dealt with the top priority of getting back into production by reviving its prewar Series E 8hp and Series M 10hp models.

There were almost certainly other reasons for the delay in getting the project moving again, however. One of them was that, by all accounts, senior management at Cowley were very lukewarm about the whole thing. They could see that the revived prewar cars were selling well enough, and could therefore see no urgency to get a new model into the showrooms to replace them. The fact that the Series E and Series M were distinctly old-fashioned designs seemed to be of little concern. As for Lord Nuffield himself, he had taken an instant dislike to the Mosquito when it was first shown to him, dismissing it with the remark that it looked like a poached egg.

Fortunately, Issigonis and the Mosquito had one staunch supporter in the shape of Miles Thomas, the Vice-Chairman of the Nuffield Organisation. He was not afraid to stand up to Lord Nuffield, and in the end it cost him his job. Thomas resigned in the autumn of 1947, and his place was taken by Reggie Hanks, a rather less forthright man who was nevertheless also a strong supporter of Issigonis and the Mosquito. As a result, just one battle was lost as the Mosquito progressed from prototype to production. That was over the engine, and ironically enough both Issigonis and Miles Thomas made their own contributions towards the defeat.

The British car taxation system had for many years been based on a formula established by the Royal Automobile Club, and the determining factor in that formula was the diameter of the engine's cylinder bores. Essentially, narrow bores attracted lower tax rates than wide bores, with the result that engines designed in Britain tended to have long strokes to compensate for their narrow bores. This in turn inhibited engine design to a large extent, because long-stroke engines cannot be made to rev as freely as short-stroke engines, and because long-stroke engines must inevitably be fairly tall.

In the 1946 General Election, a Labour Government came into power. The Board of Trade under Sir Stafford Cripps

William Morris, later Lord Nuffield, was the founder of Morris Motors but was never a friend of the postwar Minor.

began to lean very heavily on motor manufacturers, insisting that they should sell a very high proportion of their products overseas in order to earn revenue for a Britain which had been bankrupted by the war. The car makers found this difficult, as they had never paid much attention to overseas sales in previous years and the designs they had previous constraints, British car makers now began to design much more efficient engines, while back at Cowley the need for Issigonis' two flat-four engine sizes of 800cc and 1,100cc in the Mosquito inevitably came under discussion.

This was probably just the final nail in the flat-four engine's coffin, however. In fact, there were two other factors which had made its continued existence questionable. The first was that the engine was still suffering from vibration problems which needed to be developed out. The second was that the Morris Engines Branch in Coventry were pretty unenthusiastic about building this curious new engine. The net result was that Issigonis was told to abandon his flat-four design and to use the 918cc in-line four-cylinder which was already in production. He was not happy about the idea; nor was he happy when he found that it would have to be the 27bhp side-valve version from the Morris Series E 8hp rather than the 33bhp overhead-valve version from the small-volume

Alec Issigonis, designer of the postwar Minor, was later also responsible for the Mini and several BMC front-wheel-drive cars of the Sixties. He was knighted for his services to British industry.

in production were not best suited to overseas conditions. So Miles Thomas went to see Hugh Dalton, the Chancellor of the Exchequer, and explained to him that British car makers would have far greater success abroad if they could make short-stroke, big-bore engines which delivered the power characteristics demanded in overseas markets. It would not be cost-effective to build narrow-bore engines for the British market as well, so did the Chancellor not agree that big-bore engines should be freed from punitive taxes in Britain? To help illustrate the engineering points behind the argument, Thomas took Alec Issigonis along with him.

Hugh Dalton saw the point, and swiftly abolished the RAC horsepower rating, introducing instead a flat-rate annual road tax for all cars in Britain. Freed of their

The Series M Ten was the first unitary-construction Morris, and was the first Morris on which Issigonis worked. It was introduced in 1938, and production continued through to 1948, with a break during the war years.

Issigonis was forever doodling, and here are just a few of the countless sketches he produced as his fertile brain went to work on the detail design of the Minor. The low-mounted headlamps would go through into production, but the narrow body would be widened and the grille design changed.

Wolseley Eight. Nevertheless, the in-line engine was tried in the engine bay of a prototype of the new small car some time in 1947 and, with some minimal modification to the steering gear, it fitted and it worked. So the flat-four disappeared from the specification.

Before the flat-four was abandoned, however, a further five prototypes of the new car had been built at Cowley. Whether these can properly be called Mosquitoes or not is open to question; certainly Issigonis himself always thought of the first car as the only Mosquito and the rest as Minors. That name-change had come about, by the way, because Lord Nuffield objected to the Mosquito name. Far better, he argued, to revive the name he had thought of for the 1928-1934 small Morris which had so successfully challenged the dominance of the Austin Seven in the small-car market of the day. One way or another, the issue of

what those prototypes should be called is not really clear, because only the two final examples, built in 1948 with 918cc engines, actually carried the Minor code letters of SMM, while the others retained the old SX code also used for the 1943 Mosquito prototype.

The five 1946-1947 prototypes were numbered from EX/SX/130 to EX/SX/134. The first two were completed in September 1946, the second two in January 1947, and the last one in April 1947. This last car is the only one known for certain to have had an 1,100cc flat-four engine, and EX/SX/132 from the January batch was probably the first car to be tried with a 918cc side-valve type. This car was also the first Tourer (convertible) to be built, and the arrival of a second body style demonstrates how seriously the Minor was being considered for production by the beginning of 1947. There was, however, one more stage for the car to

The Series E Morris Eight was the source of the engine which eventually went into the production Minor.

go through before the definitive Minor would emerge.

Alec Issigonis was not happy with the Minor's appearance. Stung perhaps by Lord Nuffield's jibe about the car looking like a poached egg, he had reached the conclusion by late 1947 that the car was too tall and narrow. According to legend, he therefore had one of the prototypes cut down the middle longitudinally, and had the two halves moved apart until he was satisfied with the result. Reg Job then had to re-do the body drawings to incorporate the extra 4 inches which Issigonis insisted should be inserted in the car's width. To save time – and to minimize the cost, because many of the press tools for the body had already been made – Job simply added a flat section of 4 inches right down the car's middle. The only place on the bodyshell where this could be seen was the bonnet, which now had a raised styling feature along its length. However, the bumpers and valances had already been manufactured in quantity, and so Job arranged for them to be cut in half and for metal joining

strips to be inserted to make up the extra 4 inches of overall width. It is astonishing that nobody commented on the strange appearance which resulted when the car was announced a year later.

The final two prototypes were put together in June 1948 (EX/SMM/144) and September 1948 (EX/SMM/145). Both were definitely called Minors (the SMM code was the one allocated to the Minor), and it seems pretty certain that both had 918cc side-valve engines. By this time, everything was in place for the Minor to enter full production as a replacement for the Morris Series E 8hp, and the car was announced to the public at the 1948 Motor Show in October. Lord Nuffield never did like it, and Alec Issigonis (by then Sir Alec) later recounted that the Chairman hardly ever exchanged more than a few words with him. When the production of the millionth Minor was being celebrated some 12 years later, however, Nuffield did have the good grace to say, "Thank you."

CHAPTER 2

The side-valve Minors

Series MM, 1948-1952

Nuffield Metal Products in Birmingham started building the bodyshells for the new Minor in July 1948; assembly of the first production saloon was completed at Cowley on September 20; and assembly of the first production Tourer was completed on October 14. An example of each was prepared for the Morris stand at the Earls Court Motor Show which opened towards the end of October, while production of the showroom examples got into its stride.

For a few months, the old Series E Morris 8hp models were assembled alongside the new Series MM Minors, the last one being signed off in November 1948. So it was all change on the assembly lines at Cowley for a time, as the workforce became accustomed to building the new models. In fact, Cowley must have been in a state of complete turmoil, because the Minor was not the only new Morris to appear during October 1948.

The fact that the Minor was Morris' major success story of the time tends to make us forget the other new models which were introduced alongside it. Yet it's quite important to remember that, for the Cowley management at least, the Minor was actually the least significant of the new models announced in October 1948. Far more important than a small car which they saw as designed for basic motoring were the two bigger Morris saloons, the 1½-litre MO-series Oxford and the 2.2-litre MS-series Six. With hindsight, though, it's interesting to note that the two larger cars had styling which bore quite a strong family resemblance to the Minor; so despite Lord Nuffield's "poached egg" jibe, the lines which Issigonis had drawn up were already making an impact on the whole of the Morris range.

These three new cars swept away the two revived prewar Morris models and announced the company's intention of moving back into the six-cylinder market where Nuffield had been represented only by Wolseley in the immediate postwar years. There were Wolseley editions of the two larger models, too, the 4/50 being an upmarket Morris Oxford and the 6/80 an upmarket Morris Six. Yet there was no upmarket Wolseley edition of the Minor, even though both this and an MG version had been considered in 1946; the postwar Wolseley Eight, which was Lord Nuffield's favourite car in his old age, disappeared and was not replaced.

So there was every reason for Nuffield management to think that the Minor would be more or less ignored as a bread-and-butter car and would remain in the shadow of the splendid new big Morrises and Wolseleys. Not a bit of it, though. In fact, the response to the bigger cars was rather lukewarm and all the enthusiasm was reserved for the Minor! The press were impressed: "a real triumph of British design," said *The Autocar*, while *The Motor* spoke of the "very substantial all-round progress" which the car's design represented. It seems pretty clear that the Minor was the star of the 1948 Earls Court Show, which says a lot for the car when you realize that it was up against some extraordinarily glamorous competition in the shape of Jaguar's stunning new XK120 sports model.

It quickly became clear that Nuffield had underestimated demand for the Minor. Sales of the Morris Series E 8hp

which it directly replaced had averaged out at around 20,000 a year, and so Nuffield had assumed that the Minor would sell in the same sort of quantities. The original production plans therefore allowed for around 400 cars a week, but this very quickly had to be increased to 600 a week. Even that wasn't enough to satisfy demand, and before long Nuffield found itself hastily constructing new buildings to house the additional lines needed to put Minor production up to 1,000 cars a week. Morris found itself celebrating production of the 10,000th Minor a lot earlier than it had expected, early in 1951. Nor was that the peak: in later years, shift working and other measures would enable as many as 3,000 Minors to be turned out in a week – more than seven times the original 1948 production estimate!

The old Series E had been available both as a two-door saloon and as a four-door saloon, and before the war as an open Tourer as well. Work had started on a four-door edition of the Minor as soon as the two-door saloon had been signed-off in 1946, but Nuffield management had considered it more important to get an open car back into its range. This was the reason why only two-door saloon and two-door Tourer versions of the Minor were announced at the 1948 show.

Even though potential customers who saw the new models at the show welcomed them enthusiastically, the majority knew that there was little chance of getting their hands on one. Clement Attlee's Labour Government was still urging British manufacturers to export their products in order to earn foreign revenue, which in effect meant that priority had to be accorded to orders from overseas. Morris did as it was urged, and of the 28,590 Minors built in the first full year of production, only about 25% (roughly 7,150) remained in Britain. For 1950, just over 80% of the 48,061 cars built were exported, leaving around 9,610 for Britain. Then for 1951, the export figure amounted to nearly 90% of the 48,341 cars assembled, so that only some 4,850 cars were available for sale through British showrooms. The Government's policy was not relaxed until 1952, and so it was not until then that the Minor could establish its natural

The original 'low-light' design, with the headlamps alongside the grille, lasted only for two years. Clearly visible in this picture is the fillet inserted in the front bumper to bridge the gap created when the car was widened at the last minute, after the bumpers had been made.

level of sales through the dealer network in Britain.

Of course, Morris Motors did not complain about their new car's success overseas, even if the would-be British customer might have muttered a bit. The fact that it did have such great appeal outside its native country spoke volumes for the soundness of its design; many British designers were still rather insular in their outlook and could not understand why what was good for British tastes did not appeal to Johnny Foreigner. According to Paul Skilleter's history of the Minor, the car's biggest overseas markets were Australia and the USA, in that order, followed by Eire, South Africa and New Zealand, all roughly level-pegging in terms of sales volume. Next came Canada – no surprises here – but after that came Sweden, Holland, Malaya and Denmark. It was pretty clear that the car was selling not only in those territories with traditional links to Britain (such as the Commonwealth countries), but also in markets where it was having to fight on equal terms with the products of other nations. This, truly, was success.

For a variety of reasons, though, not all these Series MM Minors were actually assembled in Britain. Some overseas countries restricted imports in exactly the same way as Britain was doing at the time, taxing some goods so heavily that they were priced out of the market. Road vehicles were particularly affected, as many countries sought to protect their domestic industries or to make money from the import of necessities. As a cheap car, the Minor was very vulnerable in such a climate, as heavy taxation removed its *raison d'être*. So Nuffield got around the problem by arranging for Minors to be shipped abroad in kit form for assembly in the country of destination.

This satisfied the overseas governments, who recognized that the assembly operations provided work for their own people, and that the provision of locally-manufactured items such as tyres, electrical components and soft trim brought activity to their own economies. Minors were therefore shipped out in CKD (Completely Knocked Down) form for assembly in South Africa, Eire, the Netherlands, Denmark, New Zealand, Australia and India. The first of these operations to start up was British Car

17

The Minor had a fairly squat stance for a small saloon of its day, but without those extra inches in the middle it would have looked tall and narrow.

Assemblers in Durban, South Africa, towards the end of 1949.

The Series MM two-door saloons, 1948-1951

So what exactly were these cars which enjoyed such phenomenal success, to the surprise of their maker's management? They were known as the Series MM models (the significance of those two letters should be readily apparent), and they came as two-door saloons or two-door Tourers. Let's look first at the saloons, which outsold the Tourers by a very considerable margin. Exact figures aren't available, but at a guess the saloons accounted for 80-85% of all Series MM Minors built between 1948 and 1951, when only the two original models were on sale.

The saloon bodyshell was very much as Issigonis had originally wanted it, complete with headlamps mounted low down alongside the radiator grille. The designer's intention had been to preserve the smooth lines of the wings by keeping the lamps recessed into the front panel, and in fact he is said to have described the later restyling which put the lamps on top of the wings as an act of vandalism! The production grille, preceded by many attempts to find a satisfactory style, had ended up as a rather fussy chromed affair with both vertical and horizontal bars. A split windscreen was still in the specification, as it had been on the original Mosquito of 1943, and Morris had taken advantage of the fact to provide the Minor with a single windscreen wiper on the driver's side: buyers who wanted one for the passenger's side as well had to pay extra!

These very first cars had some interesting features which quickly disappeared from the specification. Not least among them was a single circular tail-lamp on the offside rear wing, matched on the nearside by nothing more than a red reflector. If this was an attempt to save manufacturing costs in the same vein as the single windscreen wiper, it must have been counterbalanced by the hand-painted coachline which ran along the bodyside moulding and by a matching line painted on each road wheel. The first Minors built for the home market also had the dip-and-switch headlamp system then demanded by British law, which extinguished the offside lamp and dipped the nearside one. More

The interior of the original Minor was distinctively different from those which came later. These are the seats of NWL 576, again pictured by Robert Hawkins.

expensive cars had a centrally-mounted 'pass lamp' which filled in the darkness which descended when the headlamps were switched from main beam; sadly, the Minor had no such fitting and a pass lamp was not even offered as an accessory. Cars for export, however, had the much more effective and much safer double-dipping system.

Inside the car, passengers sat in far less Spartan conditions than might have been expected for a small car in 1948. The Minor had no pretensions to luxury, of course, but there was reasonable legroom in the back and the two individual front seats were really rather comfortable. Upholstery was in ICI's new hard-wearing Vynide, and although the colour-range was restricted to beige (with a variety of contrasting pipings) the general interior ambience was very pleasant.

The driver was faced with a large three-spoke steering wheel, and behind it was a single speedometer dial. That was flanked by rectangular gauges which indicated the petrol tank's contents and the engine oil pressure, and all three gauges had black digits on white faces, together with red pointers. The dashboard – all metal, and painted in a rather attractive gold – was designed to suit both RHD and LHD cars without modification, and in its centre was a chrome-barred grille which looked as if it had been transplanted from an American car. Underneath this were unlabelled Bakelite switches. The left and right halves of the dash were mirror images of one another, and the circular cut-out for the speedometer ahead of the driver was mirrored by a circular cut-out directly ahead of the

Alec Issigonis never did approve of the revised frontal styling which resulted when the headlamps were moved to the wing crowns. It has to be said, though, that the stylists made a very good job of what had become a necessity if the car was to be sold in the USA. The painted ring on the wheel centres was abandoned when the 'high-headlamp' models entered production, and new hubcaps with an 'M' motif were fitted; this car must be an early styling prototype.

passenger on the glovebox lid. Normally, this was plugged with a large plastic Morris emblem, but buyers could order a Smith's clock as an optional extra to replace it, and in Britain at least this became a popular purchase.

The engine and gearbox were almost pure Morris Series E items. As explained in the previous chapter, Alec Issigonis' proposed flat-four engine had been rejected in favour of the existing production in-line four-cylinder engine of 918cc. In all honesty, this was a good choice from the production engineers' point of view, but not from the customers'. It was an ancient side-valve unit which dated back in its essentials to 1934 and had been slightly modified in 1938 when the Series E was introduced. It had actually been designed for the original Morris Minor – which until 1934 had an overhead-camshaft in-line four of 847cc – and had been copied more or less directly from the 933cc engine of the 1932 Ford Model Y. With an ancestry like that, it had nothing much to be proud of, although there was no doubt that it was a tried and tested engine of proven reliability.

Its age showed in a number of ways, however. The cooling system was very much out of date for the late Forties, being a thermo-syphon type which depended on having a head of water in the radiator above the highest point on the engine. There was no water pump, and as a result it was not possible to fit these early Minors with a heater. It was true that heaters were not yet expected as standard equipment on small cars, of course, but before long Morris found itself obliged to do something about this shortcoming.

The other main reminder of the engine's age – side-valve configuration and all-iron construction apart (though Morris did fit an alloy sump) – lay in the way in performed. It gave the Minor saloon a top speed of around 60mph, which was adequate for a small car of the time, but acceleration left something to be desired. "Dazzling performance is not compatible with extreme economy," as *The Motor* so tactfully put it when reviewing the new Minor in its issue dated October 27, 1948, "but there is brisk acceleration if the four-speed gearbox is used freely." That gearbox was, of course, also an elderly design, lacking synchromesh on bottom gear. Still, it did at least come with a handily-placed floor change lever, which can only have been an improvement over the column-change which Issigonis had wanted back in 1943.

The professionals of the motoring press liked the car a lot, despite its shortcomings. *The Autocar* argued that the car "has a general feeling of liveliness on the road much beyond what may be suggested by the acceleration figures taken by the stopwatch" – and that after obtaining a set of acceleration figures which later examples suggested were way below par. That magazine's road-test staff also drew attention to the Minor's "many attributes", and singled out two in particular for detailed praise. "First, a suspension which, for smooth and even riding comfort, and remarkable stability on curves and corners, is first rate, and doubly an achievement on a small car. Second, a steering which is light, and quick, and accurate."

All that was true enough. Driving one of these very early Minors on A-roads and B-roads today, you tend to forget the car's age because its steering, brakes and general demeanour do not present a handicap. Only in outright acceleration is the car in any way deficient when compared to more modern small cars. Of course, a side-valve Minor is not a car for modern motorway conditions. Expecting a car just capable of 60mph to hold its own in traffic which for the most part is travelling at 80-90mph despite a 70mph speed limit is expecting too much!

The Series MM Tourers, 1948-1951
What, then, of the Tourers which were contemporary with these first Series MM saloons? Basically, they were two-door saloons with the roof and upper pillars removed behind the windscreen, although that of course is not how they were built. Tourer bodies had certain special features in their construction, all designed to compensate for the loss of stiffening which came from the roofless configuration.

Starting at the front, the dash panel was braced to the A-posts to reduce scuttle-shake when the car was driven over rough surfaces. Next, the box-section sills at the outer edges of the floorpan were reinforced. Finally, the B-posts were braced to the top of the inner sill by small brackets. That was it, though – the basic strength of the Minor's monocoque was such that no more reinforcement was needed. You might argue that the shell must therefore have

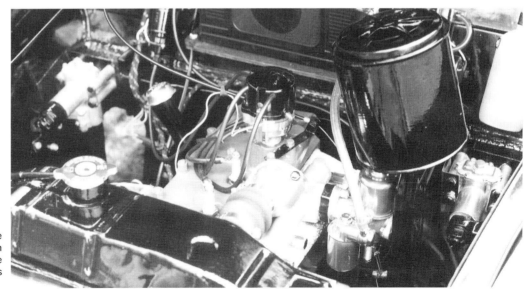

The 918cc side-valve engine of the Series MM Minor was inherited from the old Morris Eight, and never gave the car the sort of performance its 'chassis' could handle.

been over-engineered, and you would be right, but without that over-engineering there would be fewer Minors around for enthusiasts to enjoy today!

Leaving aside a simple tipping mechanism on the front seat frames which allowed passengers to get into and out of the back seat, the interior of the Tourer was much the same as that of the saloon. To give maximum room to rear seat passengers, the folding canvas roof had been arranged to sit on top of the rear body when open, and the metal arms which supported it and pivoted from the body sides were thin enough not to take away valuable shoulder-room. Tourers had the standard winding windows in their front doors, but there was no fixed glass above the rear quarters. Instead, there were detachable sidescreens which could be folded and stowed in the boot.

Hood, sidescreens and hood bag were invariably finished in beige, and the hood bag invariably failed to fit properly. What the driver could see out of the tiny rear window when the hood was up would not help him very much in assessing the behaviour of the following traffic, and for that reason many cars were fitted with oversize rear windows in later years when their hoods wore and needed replacement. Nevertheless, the Tourer was a relatively snug and weatherproof car with the top up, and with the top down it gave driver and passengers a delightful open-air motoring experience.

Production changes, 1949-1950

In the two years between the Minor's introduction and the addition to the range of a four-door saloon model, a number of running changes were made in production. It was in March 1949 that the last car was finished with the original cellulose paint, as Morris switched to synthetics on the production lines, and in the same month the nearside rear red reflector was replaced by a stop/tail lamp to match the existing one on the offside. Then in June 1949, these little round lamps were replaced by larger items with protruding lenses which were roughly triangular when viewed from the side. Chromed window frames were superseded by painted ones in December 1949 (they were cheaper!), the facia switches benefited from identifying

letters in February 1950, and then from July that year the saloons were given two sun visors as standard equipment.

Many Minor enthusiasts don't realize that the first cars with the raised or wing-mounted headlamps were built in this period. In fact, trials with high-mounted lamps were being carried out at Cowley as early as September 1948, and one of the original 'narrow' Minor prototypes was used as the guinea-pig. It wasn't that the company was having second thoughts about the styling, though. The fact was that the state of California in the USA had decided to introduce new regulations about headlamp position. All new cars sold there from October 1, 1949 would have to have their headlamps a certain height above the ground, and the Minor's were too low to comply.

Although Morris probably couldn't have predicted how well the Minor would sell in the USA, even at this stage the company was keen to try hard in that market. So the front wings were modified to accept headlamps in new fairings which blended into their front faces and into the wing crowns, and Morris took the opportunity to replace the original 5-inch headlamps with the new 7-inch type which Lucas hoped to make an industry standard. The sidelights, which were simply additional bulbs in the headlamp bowls of the 5-inch lamps, were now made separate items alongside the grille.

So from January 1949, Minors exported to the USA had high-mounted 7-inch headlamps with separate sidelights, while cars for every other part of the world had the original 1948 lighting configuration. The result was a relatively small number of cars unique in the Minor story, because they had the original 'split' bumpers and valances but the high-mounted headlamps generally associated with the later cars. The high-mounted lamps did not remain unique to the USA for long, though, and from October 1950 they became available for the rest of the world on the new four-door Minor saloon.

The Series MM four-door saloons

As we've already seen, Morris had been thinking about a four-door Minor as long as two years before the car hit the showrooms. It took four years for the plan to become reality, and the four-door Minor was introduced as a companion model to the two-door saloon and Tourer at the Earls Court Show in 1950 as a 1951 model. Four-door Minors were available only for export at first, though, and once again those would-be customers living in Britain who had seen the car at the show were obliged to wait before they could buy one.

Apart from the obvious differences of the four-door configuration, the new model introduced some novelties which would later find their way onto the two-door saloons and the Tourer. The high-mounted headlamps were one; twin wipers as standard were a most welcome addition, and so were an interior light, self-cancelling trafficators, and windscreen demister ducts in the facia. The four-doors also had smart stainless steel window frames, and a bright escutcheon just behind each exterior door handle. Rear door armrests, strap-type door-pulls, and swivelling ashtrays in the front door trims were further refinements which helped to justify the new model's increased price.

At long last, Morris was running out of supplies of the original 'split' bumpers and valances, so the four-doors had new single-piece items all round. They also had thinner coachlines on their bodyside mouldings, no coachline on their wheels, and new hubcaps with an 'M' motif in the centre. Semaphore trafficators mounted high up on the B/C posts were an additional benefit, being much more visible to following drivers than the low-mounted trafficators of the two-door cars. These, of course, never would find their way onto the two-doors, for the very good reason that there was nowhere to put them.

If the four-door was a much-appreciated addition to the range, it did have one major drawback. It was some 5cwt (560lb, 254kg) heavier than its two-door sister, and the arthritic old side-valve engine could barely take the strain. Contemporary road-tests commented on the fact, and there isn't any doubt that you can still feel the difference today if you drive examples of both types, one after the other. It was becoming increasingly clear that the Minor needed a new engine – but the one it eventually got was not one which anyone could have predicted when the car was new in 1948.

Later Series MM models had this type of chromed badging on the bonnet sides. The painted coachline is missing from this example.

Production changes, 1950-1953

The interior modifications introduced on the four-door Minor filtered down to the two-door saloon and the Tourer in October and November 1950, although the original low-mounted headlamps and the split bumpers and valances lingered on until the following January. The three models then remained in production until February 1953 (although the last Series MM four-door was made the previous month). For their final eight months, they were being built alongside the new overhead-valve Series II Minors which were introduced for export only in July 1952.

Some important engine changes were introduced towards the end of 1950. First of all, the trend towards better oil filtration arrangements was reflected in the adoption of an external oil filter in place of the one fitted inside the sump. That occurred during October, and then in December came a more thoroughly revised engine which incorporated an

The early cars had no escutcheon behind the door handles. This two-door shows the later type of handle and the semaphore trafficator let into the body side.

From 1954, new lighting regulations in the UK demanded red reflectors at the rear. This aftermarket installation was typical of the times.

impeller-type water pump. This, of course, made it possible to fit a Smith's heater, which was made standard for the USA but an extra-cost option everywhere else. Morris also introduced a conversion kit which enabled owners of earlier cars to fit a water pump and heater. The new engine carried the type-code of UHSM3; the earlier one had always been a UHSM2 since the start of Minor production in 1948.

Even as late as 1951, the materials shortages which had

This badge in the glovebox lid could be replaced by a clock at extra cost.

January 1952, losing their door-mounted ashtrays at the same time. From May 1952, a secondary steering damper was added to reduce unwanted movement transmitted to the steering wheel through the still very direct rack-and-pinion system.

Meanwhile, the Tourer had been renamed as a Convertible in June 1951. This was not merely a renaming exercise, though. Morris had made the car a tad more sophisticated and modern by scrapping the original detachable sidescreens and substituting fixed glass windows above the rear body sides. The hood was altered to suit, although its basic shape remained unaltered. The result was

This period radio complements the dash of an early Series MM.

been such a feature of the early postwar years still occurred from time to time, and in March there was a sudden shortage of nickel. Morris accordingly stopped nickel-plating hubcaps and radiator grilles, painting the grilles in grey or body-colour and the hubcaps in black. Plated hubcaps returned in September, but the grilles remained painted from now on, although plated ones were available as an extra-cost item. Right in the middle of this nickel shortage, Morris announced that four-door models would have overriders as standard (from April 1951), but astonishingly the overriders were always delivered with a plated finish.

It was in August 1951 that all the bonnets on all models were modified, being lengthened backwards to give a shorter scuttle panel at the base of the windscreen. Then the end of the year saw the two-door saloons and the open cars given a swivelling ashtray in the centre of the facia's grille. The four-doors picked up the same modification in a rather more weatherproof car, although it's arguable that the Convertible lost some of the charm of the earlier Tourer because it was no longer possible to have completely open-top motoring.

Quicker Minors

When the Series MM Minors were new, it was very clear to many people that their 'chassis' could handle a lot more power than the elderly side-valve engine could dish out in standard form. Even Morris tried out the overhead-valve Wolseley Eight engine in some prototypes during 1951, but any plans there may have been to put this into production cars were overtaken by events. So it was left to aftermarket tuners to come up with power improvements for the car.

It is probable that all manner of power improvements were being cooked up by DIY mechanics in the early Fifties, but there were just three commercially-available conversions which are worth looking at. According to *The Motor* road test, you could get a Series MM Minor up to 73mph by fitting the Alta overhead-valve conversion, which consisted of a bolt-on alloy cylinder head and neat new valve-gear driven by the original camshaft. Racing driver Stirling Moss was probably the most famous owner of the Derrington 'Silvertop' conversion, which retained the original side valves but added an alloy cylinder head and twin SU carburettors. That would take a Minor beyond 75mph, but if you wanted an 80mph top speed you had to bolt on a Shorrocks supercharger. In theory, that could be used in conjunction with either the Alta or the Derrington conversion, but whether the engine lasted very long when it was is another question!

All of these conversions are highly sought-after by enthusiasts today, but they are also very rare. It is also worth pointing out that a supercharged side-valve Minor is still no match for a modern small family car, either in straight-line acceleration or in roadholding and handling!

This 1950 Minor Tourer was owned by my publisher in the mid-Fifties until the day it proved so slow on a long uphill test on a rally that he decided the time had come to exchange it for something more powerful. Nevertheless, he still retains fond memories of it.

CHAPTER 3

The Series II Minors

Saloons, Convertibles and Travellers, 1952-1956

If there was one thing that was wrong with the Series MM Minor, it was its performance. The car handled brilliantly by the standards of the time, and it clung to the road better than any other Morris product of the late Forties. Sadly, though, its acceleration was bordering on the pathetic and its maximum speed of 62mph only adequate.

Morris resolved to do something about this at the earliest opportunity, and during 1951 the idea of fitting the overhead-valve Wolseley version of the 918cc engine seems to have been revived. According to Jack Daniels, who was still closely involved with the Minor at this stage, the transplant was very successful. It's doubtful whether the Nuffield production engineers would have been very keen on restarting manufacture of an engine which had been out of production since 1948, but as things were to turn out the issue never had to be resolved. Changes on a broader scale were about to take place at Morris Motors as the Fifties got under way in earnest.

What happened next had its roots in the middle Thirties, when Lord Nuffield fell out with Leonard Lord, whom he had appointed as Managing Director of Morris Motors at Cowley. Lord had spent four years, from 1932 to 1936, rejuvenating the Morris product line and updating the assembly processes, and was understandably extremely angry at Nuffield's refusal to grant him a proportion of the extra profits his skill had generated. In August 1936, he walked out of Nuffield's office swearing to get his own back. Some 18 months later, he was appointed works director at the Longbridge plant of Nuffield's biggest rival, Austin. If the war had not intervened, it is pretty certain that there would have been fireworks between the two companies before long.

Meanwhile, Leonard Lord quickly made his way up the corporate ladder at Austin. In 1945, he became its Chairman and Chief Executive, which at least put him on a par with Lord Nuffield as the head of a major motor manufacturer. The time was not yet right for him to exact his revenge, though. The Government's export drive in the late Forties favoured co-operation rather than competition between motor manufacturers in Britain, and in October 1948 Lord and Nuffield issued an extraordinary joint statement which said that their two companies had reached "an arrangement whereby there is to be a constant interchange of information on production methods, costs, purchases, design and research, patents and all other items which would be likely to result in manufacturing economies. The object is to effect maximum standardization, coupled with the most efficient manufacture, and by the pooling of all factory resources, a consequent reduction of costs."

These were brave ideas, expressed in language which was designed to suggest that Austin and the Nuffield Organisation had the best interests of the British economy at heart. The reality was rather different, though. Leonard Lord and Lord Nuffield were barely on speaking terms at this stage, and the rivalry between their two companies was such that co-operation at shop-floor level was going to be a difficult business to achieve. So nothing of any major

One feature instantly identifies this two-door Minor as a Series II model from the side – the chromed 'handle' at the leading edge of the bonnet.

importance happened, and just nine months later, in July 1949, the agreement was ended.

That would have been that but for Lord's determination and the intercession of Carl Kingerlee, Lord Nuffield's personal secretary. Kingerlee believed that a merger between Austin and the Nuffield Organisation was in the best interests of both companies, and he managed to get Leonard Lord and Lord Nuffield talking towards the end of 1950. The two reached agreement, but Nuffield was baulked by his Board of Directors and the merger was put off. According to legend, Lord then openly declared war on Nuffield by commissioning the tooling for the new baby Austin which was to fight for Morris Minor sales; in fact, the A30 had been planned for some time, but the story does

at least conjure up the atmosphere of the times. Leonard Lord made a further approach to Nuffield, and this time, Nuffield rode roughshod over his Directors and formally agreed to a merger. The implications of the move were masked by the choice for the merged companies of a new name (the British Motor Corporation or BMC), but there was no doubt about what had actually happened. Lord had got his hands on the Nuffield Organisation and from now on Austin would be the dominant partner.

BMC came into existence on March 31, 1952, and the effect on the Morris Minor was almost immediate. Trials of the Wolseley-engined Minor prototypes were abandoned, and the Morris engineers were instructed to fit the overhead-valve engine from the Austin A30 into the Minor.

Dates are difficult to establish, but it looks as if the first Minor prototypes with A-series engines were built around May 1952. The installation seems to have been problem-free, and the first overhead-valve Minors rolled off the production lines at Cowley in August 1952. They were four-door saloons, intended for export markets only, and they were known as Series II models. The Series MM side-valve cars remained in production beside them for a few months longer, but after February 23, 1953, the OHV Minor took over completely.

The A-series engine and gearbox
Diehard Morris fans will have to forgive a further digression into Austin history here, but the engine which BMC decided to fit into the Series II Minor to replace the ageing side-valve Morris type was, after all, an Austin design. With a swept volume of 803cc, it was actually the smallest British car engine in production in 1952, and it was, of course, considerably smaller than the 918cc Morris side-valve. Nevertheless, its more modern overhead-valve design allowed it to produce more power than the engine in the Series MM Minors – 30bhp as against 27.5bhp – and it had a first-class reputation for durability and economy. So good was its basic design, in fact, that the engine's relatives remained in production in various British-built cars until the early Nineties.

The overhead-valve engine first saw production in 1951 for the new Austin Seven, or A30, the car with which Leonard Lord hoped (in vain, as it turned out) to demolish the Morris Minor's market lead. However, its design can be traced back to the 1947 Austin A40 Devon and its 1,200cc four-cylinder engine. That was an important engine in many ways because it became the ancestor of the generally bigger B-series engines which served BMC through the Fifties and Sixties, and it also sired the smaller A-series engine of the A30.

Austin had originally wanted a new side-valve engine for the car they intended should replace the prewar Seven, and it wasn't until 1949 that plans for this were scrapped in favour of building a scaled-down version of the acclaimed

The 803cc A-series engine completely transformed the Minor's performance when it was put into the Series II. What a pity BMC didn't make a little more effort with the gearbox, though!

Austin A40 type. Austin's designers used the same bore-to-stroke ratio, although both bore and stroke were smaller in the new engine, and they used the same neat and simple layout. This meant that all the electrical components (starter, dynamo, distributor and spark plugs) were on one side of the engine, while the camshaft, pushrods, inlet ports and exhaust ports were all on the other side. In addition, they called on the services of tuning expert Harry Weslake to design the combustion chamber. Weslake's main contribution was to optimize the gas-flow and to provide very efficient combustion by using concave piston crowns and carefully-shaped valve ports. His original plans called for an alloy cylinder head, but for a variety of reasons the production engines were of all-iron design.

The first 803cc engine was ready for the test-bed in March 1950, and one was running in a prototype A30 by December. When it went into production during 1951, it was known as the AS3 engine, but under BMC its title was shortened to A-series – and that was what it was called by the time it went into the Morris Minor.

Unfortunately, the A-series gearbox which went into the Series II Minor was less of an inspired choice than the A-series engine ahead of it. Like the engine, it was transplanted straight from the Austin A30, but the ratios which had worked so well on the 1,500lb A30 were less well-suited to the 1,735lb Minor. That explains why the Minor's final-drive ratio was lowered in January 1954, although the improved acceleration which resulted was only a partial solution because the ratios remained poorly spaced. The Austin gearbox was no easier to use, either, having an unsynchronized bottom gear exactly like the original Minor gearbox.

BMC lost no time in drawing attention to the virtues of the new OHV Minor. During October 1952, some months before the car was available on the home market, a four-door example was sent on an extraordinary 'test run' (for which, please read 'publicity stunt'!) at the Goodwood motor racing circuit. There it ran non-stop for 10,000 miles over a period of 10 days, servicing and even tyre changes being carried out on the move in a specially-built trailer cage towed behind an adapted MS-series Morris Six. The engine was kept running all the time, and BMC were at pains to point out that the car covered 10,164 miles (equivalent to an average year's motoring) at an average speed of 45.3mph and an average fuel consumption of 43mpg.

The first Series II Minors
It wasn't easy to tell a Series II Minor apart from one of the superseded Series MM models unless you took your cue from the small boys of the day. They could tell the difference at a glance because the Series II models had a raised and chromed 'handle' on the leading edge of the bonnet instead of the MM's chromed flash, together with a different style of bonnet badge. With a bit more perseverance, it was possible to tell the difference by listening for the different exhaust note, too!

Of course, the fact was that the Series II Minor really wasn't all that different from the car it replaced. The profile of the bulkhead had been changed to make room for the OHV engine, but that was only visible when the bonnet was lifted, and at that point the game was already up! The first Series II cars did come with three new paint colours (Clarendon Grey, Empire Green and Birch Grey) which had not been available on the 1948-1952 MMs, but unfortunately they shared these new colours with the 1953-model MMs built alongside them. So that was no help, either.

Rather than making changes for the sake of change, BMC were concentrating on expanding the Minor range. In this they were following plans which Morris Motors had laid down earlier. First came the van and pick-up versions of the Series II models in May 1953 (which are described in Chapter 6), and next came the new Traveller model in October that year. Both had existed in prototype form long before the BMC merger.

The 1953 range expansion didn't only consist of additional body styles, though. When the 1954-model Minors were introduced in October 1953, there was also a small expansion of the range within itself. The 1953-model specification now became the entry-level standard model, and for extra cost you could buy a De Luxe version which featured leather upholstery instead of Vynide, plus the optional passenger's sun visor as standard. It sold, too: people were beginning to see in the Minor something rather more than minimal motoring on a budget.

A few further changes followed. The 1954-model Minor saloons introduced in October 1953 had fabric headlinings in place of the rather Spartan board-type linings used since 1948, and a couple of months later the front seat frames were modified. More visibly, these were accompanied by a new style of upholstery with stitching running fore-and-aft rather than from side to side. Then in January 1954 the Morris semi-floating rear axle was replaced by a three-quarters floating axle known (almost inevitably) as the BMC A-type axle. The idea was standardization and rationalization across the BMC range, but there had to be pain before there could be any gain. The axle brought with it hubs designed to take studs for mounting the road wheels, so with its introduction the original bolted rear wheels disappeared and new wheel pressings arrived. BMC took the opportunity to lower the final-drive ratio at the same time, but the results were only partially successful, as already explained. The Morris Minor Travellers introduced in October 1953 had these A-type axles with their revised gearing from the beginning.

By this stage, the first road-test reports of the Series II Minor had already appeared in the press. It was *The Autocar* which explained the new car's virtues most succinctly. "Performance tests show that the maximum speed is little changed, the latest car showing an improvement of 1mph, but there is considerable improvement in acceleration times. For example, acceleration from 10-30mph in top gear takes just over 16 secs as compared with 23.5 secs with the sidevalve engine. At the same time, there is, however, a slight drop in maximum speeds obtainable on the gears; the maximum normally used in third is now 34mph with an ultimate 42mph, whereas with the sidevalve the figures were 38mph and 46mph respectively."

The Minor Traveller

The estate car was never popular in Britain during the Thirties, and no manufacturer listed one as a regular

This style of hubcap, bearing an 'M' in its centre, came in with the four-door Series MM cars and was carried over to the Series II.

production model. Such vehicles did exist, of course, but they tended to be coachbuilt on some of the more expensive chassis of the day. Traditionally wooden-framed, they were more commonly known as Shooting Brakes, and that name gives a clue to their origin. They were intended to carry shooting parties across the large estates of the rich; the market, obviously, was therefore pretty limited.

Two things conspired to change all that. The first was that American car buyers began to see the value of large-capacity 'station wagons' during the later Thirties and, taking their cue and a certain amount of snob appeal from the British shooting brake, they gave them bodies with

The 'long bonnet', again introduced during the Series MM production run, is seen here on a 1955 Series II.

exposed wooden frames. The use of such vehicles by the American military brought examples to Britain during the war, and the vogue for all things American which followed the hostilities did the rest. Then a loophole in British taxation laws in the middle Forties encouraged small coachbuilders to construct similar wooden-framed bodies on a variety of chassis for the home market.

So by 1952, the wooden-bodied estate car was an established feature of the British motoring scene. Morris Motors capitalized on the fact that year by introducing a wooden-bodied Morris Oxford Traveller on the 1½-litre MO-series chassis, taking its name from the idea of a 'Traveller's car' (the word then suggested a travelling salesman more than anything else). In anticipation of the Oxford Traveller's popularity, work had already begun early in 1951 on a Minor-based equivalent.

When the Morris Minor Traveller was announced in October 1953 as an addition to the existing range of two-door saloon, four-door saloon, light commercials and Convertible, it therefore appeared to the buying public to be a scaled-down version of the MO-series Traveller. The exposed ash framework was both attractive and fashionable for the times (though it would appear quaint when the final Minor Travellers were built some 17 years later), and was without any doubt an important part of the car's appeal. It would certainly have been cheaper for Morris to have used a common metal body for both the Minor estate and the van which had gone into production a few months earlier; but no, wooden-framed estates were what the public wanted and so a wooden-framed Minor Traveller was what they got. Having different rear bodies also allowed Morris to give the van a higher roof and so make it more capacious.

Looking at the Minor Traveller, a buyer at the 1953 Motor Show might have been forgiven for thinking that Morris had simply bolted a wooden framework onto the back half of a four-door Minor saloon and filled in the gaps with alloy panels. There was rather more to it than that, though. To keep the whole structure rigid, Morris had actually reinforced the inner sills of the floorpan (rather differently from the way it had been done on the Convertible), and they had given the estate body a flat rear

The versatile Traveller was a welcome addition to the Minor range and was destined to account for almost exactly one-sixth of all the cars produced.

Large doors are fitted at the rear of the Traveller, and the rear seat backrest is made to fold forward to provide a large stowage area. The rear seat cushion hinges upwards to protect the backs of the front seats. A separate lower compartment contains the spare wheel and tools.

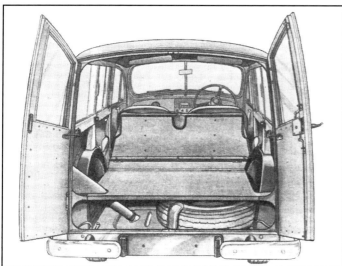

floor by modifying the floorpan to remove the curvature in the existing Minor boot area. The rear seat was hinged to fold forwards to lengthen the load floor, and overall the Traveller made a very practical dual-purpose holdall. Its buyers weren't confined to travelling salesmen, either. Many family buyers found it an immensely useful vehicle for transporting dogs or large quantities of luggage along with the children, and in those days before safety legislation it wasn't uncommon to see the back of a Minor Traveller bursting with children as Mum did the school run for all her friends and neighbours.

The 1955-model facelift
You can see BMC's strategy for the Minor evolving during the early part of the Fifties. The new engine arrived in 1952, the new body styles a year later, and then a year after that the whole Minor range was given a facelift. The end result was still called a Series II Minor, so for convenience Minor enthusiasts today refer to the pre-facelift cars as early Series

The welcoming interior of the Series II was reached by wide-opening doors, as this four-door model demonstrates.

IIs and the post-facelift examples as late Series IIs. The facelift was made in October 1954 for the 1955-model cars, and it would be another two years before the Minor underwent any more major changes. When it did, in the autumn of 1956, the result would be called a Morris Minor 1000.

For the moment, though, let's look at the 1955-season facelift. The Minor's appearance had already been changed quite radically once (when the raised-headlamp models were introduced in 1949-1950), and this was the first major change to their styling since then. It affected both the outside and the inside of the cars, and the most obvious change was to the front grille area. The original cheese-grater grille was replaced by a less fussy affair with horizontal slats, and the sidelights moved from the grille surround panel to the wing fronts. Other minor modifications were made to suit. The interior change was also a major one, for the old gold-painted dashboard disappeared in favour of a new and rather simpler type

The semaphore trafficators of the four-door Minor were mounted in the B-pillar

Compare the rear of this Series II four-door with the rear of the first Series MM pictured on page 18, and note particularly the much larger tail-lamps, the one-piece bumper and the overriders.

painted in the body colour. Following established Austin practice on the A30, it had a single instrument dial mounted in the centre, so that the same pressing could be used for both RHD and LHD models with the very minimum of alteration. It also had open gloveboxes on either side. Not everybody liked it, but it did give the Minor's interior a new and more modern character.

Running changes, 1955-1956

New lighting regulations introduced in Britain during 1954 specified that all new vehicles must have two red reflectors fitted at the rear, and that existing vehicles must have them fitted retrospectively. The Minor's single red reflector in the centre of the bootlid emblem was not enough, and so twin

Top up or top down, the Minor convertible was a particularly attractive-looking car. This preserved Series II was pictured for *Minor Monthly* magazine by Tony Aston. Although not totally standard this car wins many prizes.

This BMC publicity shot of a Series II four-door Minor shows the revised frontal styling introduced in October 1954, incorporating a new and neater grille and repositioned sidelamps.

reflectors were added from September 1954, just before the facelift models arrived. These were just an emergency measure until redesigned rear lights could be put into production, though. From December that year, new rear lights which incorporated a reflector in their lenses were fitted. The type fitted to saloons and Convertibles was a rather more rounded edition of the earlier 'triangular' light; Travellers, of course, had their own unique style.

Very little else happened before the Series II Minors ceased production in September 1956. In May that year, the beige tops of Convertibles were supplemented by alternative colours for the first time, and green and red varieties lent additional appeal to the open Minors. Then in June 1956, the front seat frames were modified once again, to give a fixed backrest on all models. Two-door saloons and Convertibles had seats hinged from the floor to allow access to the rear compartment.

American Minors

The USA continued to be a strong market for the Morris Minor, and BMC were quite happy to build special versions of the cars exclusively for that territory. Both standard and

De Luxe models were available, but they had a number of special features: a laminated windscreen and heater as standard, twin horns, flashers instead of semaphore trafficators, a foot-operated dipswitch and unique headlamp bulbs.

Epilogue

Nearly 270,000 Series II Minors were built in four years of production (and some sources suggest there were as many as 288,000), making an average annual production of 67,500 (or 72,000) cars. To those must be added well over 48,000 light commercials built between 1953 and 1956. So it is obvious from the figures just how successful the overhead-valve Minor was, easily eclipsing the side-valve models made between 1948 and 1953. BMC hadn't finished yet, though, and in 1956 they replaced the 803cc Minors with bigger-engined variants; these would be called Minor 1000, and were destined to outsell even the hugely successful Series II models.

Many early Minors were later fitted with flashing trafficators, using aftermarket kits. The neat installation here is one of the more satisfactory examples.

CHAPTER 4

The early Minor 1000s

948cc models, 1956-1962

It's important not to be too parochial when looking at the origins of the third-series Minor, the 948cc Minor 1000 introduced in October 1956 to replace the Series II models. The Minor had not been a pure Morris product since its adoption of the 803cc A-series engine in 1952, and as time went on the distinction between what was of Morris origin and what was of Austin origin within BMC would become increasingly blurred. It was during 1953 that Austin designers started to look at a new version of the A-series engine which BMC planned should replace the existing 803cc type in both the Austin A30 and the Morris Minor. The future of the two formerly rival cars was already being considered in tandem at this early stage.

Why exactly did BMC need a new version of the A-series engine? One reason was that the existing 803cc type simply wasn't up to what was being demanded of it in some quarters. Britain's motor makers had still not fully understood the implications of selling cars in overseas markets, and Austin had designed the 803cc engine for sedate driving on the rural roads of its native country. When subjected to the sort of sustained high-speed driving which was common in many of BMC's overseas markets, the all too common result was damage to the white-metal bearings. This, of course, put the BMC products at a disadvantage when compared to rival small cars like the Volkswagen Beetle, which could be driven flat-out at 60mph or more all day without adverse effects.

Then there was the fact that better-quality petrol was at last becoming available in the early Fifties after many years

of poor-quality 'pool' petrol following the 1939-1945 war. If BMC were to take advantage of the higher performance possibilities which this offered, they would need to go to higher compression ratios – and these would inevitably put an even greater strain on the white-metal bearings. There was a third consideration, too, which was that the Minor's 'chassis' could still handle a lot more than the 803cc A-series engine could throw at it. While the engine gave reasonable performance in the rather lighter A30 for which it had been designed, it had always been something of a compromise when installed in the Series II Minor.

The obvious solution to all these problems was an engine redesign incorporating a capacity increase. So, early in 1953, preliminary calculations were made for a range of A-series engines which varied in capacity from 848cc to 998cc, and by the end of October that year a 1,000cc engine with siamesed bores was under consideration. In essence, this was the engine which later emerged as the 948cc A-series, with its cylinder bores slightly reduced in diameter.

BMC knew that raising the compression ratio to make full use of the newly-available high-octane fuels would put the white-metal bearings under too much strain. So they redesigned the crankshaft to take the harder lead-indium bearings which had been tried experimentally in an 803cc engine during 1952. They increased the size of the big-end journals to give an additional margin of safety, and at the same time they added full-flow oil filtration to reduce the risk of the crankshaft being scored by the harder bearings.

Back in 1956, the quickest way of recognizing one of the new Minor 1000 models was by looking at the windscreen. These were the first cars to have the one-piece type which would remain standard for the next 15 years. It replaced the split-screen of the Series MM and Series II models.

The engine was first tried out in an Austin A30 and gave exceptional results.

The final stage of testing represented quite a milestone in BMC history. For the first time Austin and Morris road-test teams worked alongside one another as 948cc-engined Minors and Austins were put through their paces together over German autobahns in 1956. Based in Stuttgart, the teams clocked up 25,000 miles in each car in just a few weeks, driving the 260 miles to Munich and back in convoy. Each car covered between 600 and 800 miles a day, six days a week, and was taken off the road for servicing and maintenance on Sunday mornings. At the conclusion of the tests, the 948cc engine was pronounced a success, and it went into production in October that year.

Also on test on those German autobahns were a new gearbox and final drive, both of them fitted to the Austins and Morrises alike. The new gearbox contained more closely-spaced ratios than the old A-series 'box, as well as

According to the information which came with this BMC publicity shot, the Minor 1000 Traveller offered 20 cubic feet of luggage space. The BMC publicity department also seemed to think the capacity of the new engine was 950cc!

much-improved synchromesh. It also had a new remote-control shift, built into an extension on the back of the main casing, and this gave much sweeter changes than before. As for the new final drive, it was raised to a common 4.55:1; Series II Minors and the A30 Countryman had a 5.375:1 ratio while the A30 saloons had a 4.875:1 ratio. The purpose of this new and taller gearing was to ease the strain on the engine (and on the ears!) when the cars were travelling at the sustained high speeds which were so characteristic of their use in export markets.

So when the Morris Minor 1000 was announced in October 1956, its new engine, gearbox and axle were not exclusive to the car but were shared with the Austin A35 which was introduced at the same time. They certainly did make a difference, as enthusiastic contemporary road tests make abundantly clear. Demand for the new Morris 1000 quickly outstripped supply, aided no doubt by the buoyant market for economical cars which followed the 1956-1957 Suez crisis and the worries over petrol availability which went with it. By November 1957, BMC were obliged to

introduce overtime working at Cowley simply to keep up with orders, and 1958 was to prove a record year for Morris Minor sales.

Yet that 1958 record would never be surpassed. Good though the Minor 1000 was, it was also a 10-year-old design, and attractive alternatives rapidly began to appear on the market. In 1958, BMC's new Austin A40 combined practicality with sharp new styling by Farina in Italy. Then 1959 saw further in-house competition from the astonishing Mini, together with the cheap and stylish new Ford Anglia and the rather more expensive but equally stylish new Triumph Herald. By comparison, the Minor was already beginning to look a little dated, and sales began to suffer as a result. This, though, was the start of the Minor's classic period, the period when it was adopted by people who valued dependable and economical transport over stylish design; people like the District Nurse and the Vet. This was the time when the Minor first became a symbol of all that was cosy and dependable about a Britain which was changing too rapidly for comfort under the twin impacts of

a shrinking Commonwealth and the need to face fierce competition in the open markets of the wider world.

The first Minor 1000s

The new engine, gearbox and axle ratio were only part of the story behind the Morris Minor 1000, because the model differed in a number of other important respects from the Series II which it replaced. From the point of view of the car-spotting schoolboy, a Minor 1000 was immediately recognizable by its single-piece windscreen, which was actually slightly larger than the split-screen it replaced and was flanked by thinner pillars. From behind, a much enlarged rear window was the give-away (and there was a similarly enlarged rear window in the Convertible's canvas hood), while real Minor connoisseurs could spot the different rear wing design which enveloped the wheel more closely and concealed more of the inner wheelarch from view. Closer to, 'Morris 1000' badges on the bootlid and the sides of the bonnet confirmed the identification.

From the point of view of the driver and passengers, there were further important differences. Most obvious was the new facia with its lidded gloveboxes – a rather pointless piece of design as the hinged lid ahead of the driver fouled the steering column and could not be opened fully. BMC's answer to that was to recommend replacing the lid with a radio and speaker at extra cost! Then there was a new steering wheel with a dished centre, which was supposedly a safety feature long before such things became fashionable. The handbrake lever was more compact than the Series II type and sported a chromed pushbutton release, while the stubby gear lever sprouted from a more square-shaped gearbox cover introduced to suit the new gearbox itself. Seats were broadly similar to those in Series IIs, but their backrests and cushions had a flatter profile.

These were the improvements, but the news was not all good. The four-door saloons lost their rear armrests, and Minors built for the home market still had antiquated semaphore trafficators, even though flashers could be had for export (when the redundant slots in the bodywork were covered by ugly blanking plates). Turn signals of either sort

The 948cc engine of the first Minor 1000 had a large oil-bath air cleaner.

were now operated by a stalk mounted on the steering column instead of by the under-dash turn switch of the Series II models. Unfortunately, the turn signal warning light was incorporated in the stalk quadrant and was practically invisible in daylight. That stalk also doubled as a horn push and needed a good hard thump before it sounded the horn. Nobody seemed to like this, and over the next few years BMC made a number of attempts to improve the design.

Like the Series II models, the Minor 1000s were made available with both standard and De Luxe specifications. De Luxe meant overriders, leather upholstery and a heater, which was still an extra-cost option on the standard models. It was still a recirculatory type, too, which quickly induced drowsiness in the occupants of a car travelling with its windows closed to keep all the warmth inside. So BMC made available a fresh-air heater option (also available as a kit of parts to be retro-fitted to cars with only the standard heater). This consisted of an air intake behind the radiator grille which fed ducting around the heater box and provided

warm fresh air instead of warm stale air. It made a distinct improvement.

It was at the beginning of 948cc Minor production that the first cars were made with contrasting paint on wheels and grille slats. For the moment, this was not universal, although it proved popular and later became standard on Minors. From October 1956, then, cars painted in Black, Dark Green or Turquoise were delivered with wheels painted in Birch Grey, and the Black cars also had this second colour on their grille bars.

The press certainly approved of the new Minor. *The Motor* argued that, "the little car feels from the start like a thoroughbred. The rack-and-pinion steering is beautifully light and precise. The suspension is firm at speed and yet the ride is never harsh ... in fact the Minor 1000 may be summed up as the answer to those who need the economy and comfort of a traditional small saloon allied to a responsiveness and 'gameness' which has always been the prerogative of the well-bred sports cars of this world." That was praise indeed! As for the new gearbox, the comment in

The Autocar was that "the new … ratios have vastly improved the performance on the intermediate gears." The same magazine described the gearchange as "among the best on any car made today" and as "a pleasure to use." It was *The Autocar* which also commented on what would prove to be one of the most endearing characteristics of the Minor 1000, "an exhaust resonance which is quite noticeable on the overrun." Would today's enthusiasts be without that charming characteristic, which identifies an approaching Minor 1000 half a mile before you can see it?

Running changes, 1956-1960

Even before the end of 1956, Morris were making changes to the new 948cc Minor. In December, they fitted stronger swivel pin assemblies in the front suspension and a stronger bootlid handle and lock to resist break-ins. The next calendar year brought more changes, starting with an enlarged fuel tank in March, when a 6½-gallon fuel tank replaced the original 5-gallon type. This was mainly to suit overseas customers, who tended to drive rather longer distances than British Minor owners, and was achieved by extending the tank into the spare-wheel well. From April, the Traveller followed the saloons' lead by ditching its Rexine board headlining and adopting a fabric type, and then in August the Convertible lost its canvas hood to one made of plastic-covered material. For the 1958 model-year, though, the only change was a small shade for the indicator warning light on its steering-column-mounted quadrant.

Nothing further of note changed until the start of the 1959 model-year in September 1958, when courtesy light switches were fitted to the front doors of four-door saloons and to two-door saloons; Convertibles, however, had to do without. Probably more important was a change to the rear springs on saloons and Convertibles in December, when five-leaf springs (with ¼-inch leaves) replaced the seven-leaf type (with 7/32-inch leaves). This did give the softer ride which BMC wanted, but it's also arguable that it made the handling a little more woolly. Travellers and light commercials meanwhile retained the seven-leaf springs to cope with their heavier payloads.

The next round of changes came in February 1959. Under

The BMC rosette was well-known in the Fifties, and reproductions are now available.

the bonnet, a paper-element air cleaner in a saucepan-like canister replaced the earlier oil-bath type; but the other changes focused on the interior. Most obviously, there was new upholstery with wider panels on the seats. A bigger parcels shelf was also added under the dash, and the heater on De Luxe models was given a shroud painted in Pearl Grey. The finishing touch was on the glovebox lids, which now had a lining and a neat finisher. It was also in February 1959 that BMC decided to paint the road wheels and grille bars of all cars in Pearl Grey, which of course contrasted nicely with all colours except Pearl Grey itself!

Just a month later, the door check-straps were modified to allow wider opening, and BMC had another crack at

Minor mistakes: this picture shows the controversial indicator stalk on a 948cc Minor, and the driver's side glovebox lid, which fouled the steering column when open.

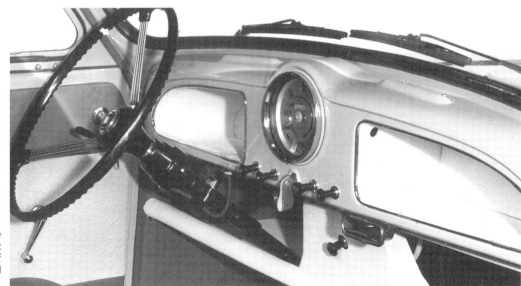

With the 1962 models – the last of the 948cc Minor 1000s – the glovebox lids disappeared. The basic shape of the dashboard nevertheless remained as it had been since 1956.

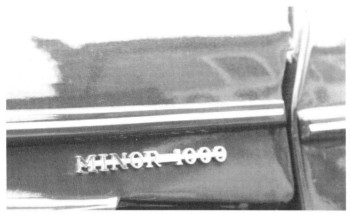

Minor 1000 badging on the bonnet and bootlid helped to distinguish the new cars.

When the semaphore trafficators were replaced by flashing indicators, this pressing remained in the B/C-post of four-door saloons.

resolving the problem of the indicator-and-horn stalk. This time, they sensibly moved the horn to the centre of the steering wheel, provided a large green indicator warning lamp on the end of the stalk, and added a self-cancelling mechanism for good measure. At last, they seemed to have got the design right.

At the 1959 Motor Show, all eyes were on the new Morris

Mini-Minor and Austin Se7en, and so BMC did very little to the Minor for the 1960 model-year. That year's cars were distinguished by a new PVC headlining, actually introduced on production in August 1959, and De Luxe models could be specified optionally with seats upholstered in nylon cloth. The survival rate of these today suggests that they were either not popular or simply did not wear well. Right-hand-drive 1960 models also had a small indentation in the gearbox cover panel to make more room for the driver's clutch foot.

These changes carried the cars through to the 1961 model-year, and there were no novelties at the start of the season in October 1960 either, although some new paint colours had been announced in July and the colour of grille bars and road wheels had been changed to Old English White. Nevertheless, BMC did have something up their sleeves for the end of the 1960 calendar-year.

The Minor Million
No British motor manufacturer had ever made a million examples of a single car until the millionth Morris Minor rolled off the assembly lines just before Christmas, 1960. For that reason, BMC decided to make a special occasion of it. The millionth car was made on December 22 and was given the special chassis number 1,000,000. Then another 349 like it were made and numbered in the special sequence 1,000,001 to 1,000,349. Of these 350 cars, 320 remained in Britain where they were first displayed at BMC showrooms before being sold to members of the public. The other 30 had left-hand drive and were sent for export; 21 of them went to the USA.

These 350 special-edition cars were known as Minor Millions, and all of them were two-door saloons painted in the same lilac colour scheme. They all wore 'Morris 1,000,000' badges on their bootlids and bonnet sides, and all of them had off-white interiors. They are highly prized by Minor enthusiasts today.

Minors for 1961 and 1962
For the 1961 model-year, the only news was the Minor Million, and it was the start of the 1962 model-year before any more changes were made to the Minor. The revised cars started coming through in August 1961, all of them now with built-in seat-belt anchorage points (though belts weren't yet mandatory except in some Scandinavian countries) and all of them – at long last – with flashing turn indicators. These were actually incorporated in the existing tail-lamps and sidelights, although the sidelights had slightly

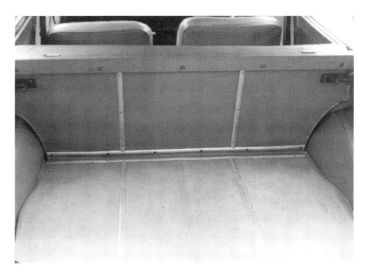

The Traveller models offered a spacious load area, which could be enlarged by folding down the rear seat backrest.

This rubber seal protected the join between the 'cab' roof and the main roof section on Travellers.

47

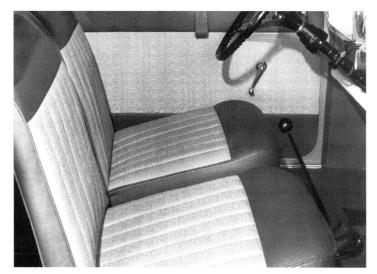

The two-toned De Luxe seats on a left-hand-drive 1962 Minor 1000.

more bulbous lenses than before to make room for the twin-filament bulbs which the new system needed.

The Motor Show in October also revealed the third style of upholstery to be seen on the 948cc Minors. This ended the use of leather upholstery on the De Luxe models, which gave way to two-toned Vynide with contrasting colour panels on the door trims as well as the seats. For the standard models, the same new style was used, but seats and door trims were all in a single colour. The heater shroud changed colour again, this time to Beige. Just too late for the show, in November, the final changes to the 948cc Minors were made as the gloveboxes lost their lids for the second time and the windscreen wipers were modified to clear a slightly bigger glass area. These cars remained in production until September 1962 when the final phase of the Minor's development opened. For many buyers of the time and enthusiasts of today, that phase was the best of them all.

The Minor Million was a commemorative special edition of 350 cars, all two-doors, finished in Lilac with white seats. BMC issued this carefully-posed publicity picture at the time.

Absolutely nothing had been restored on this 1958 two-door Minor 1000 when it was pictured by Robert Hawkins for *Minor Monthly* nearly 40 years later. Note the charming period accessories of badge bar, headlamp cowls and boot-mounted luggage rack. There is even a BMC rosette sticker on the passenger's side of the windscreen!

The thin-band whitewall tyres and left-hand-drive configuration of this Convertible are the first hints that the car is an American export model. It was pictured in Pennsylvania by Tony Aston for *Minor Monthly* magazine, and is now in the hands of an enthusiast owner.

Special Minors: US models, CKD cars and the Disabled Drivers' Minor

The later Fifties were boom years for the Morris Minor in the USA, and BMC remained ready and willing to satisfy the peculiar demands of that market. Even though the company could not be bothered to fit a keylock to the driver's door (all left-hand-drive cars had a single keylock on the passenger door – the driver's side on right-hand-drive cars!), it was prepared to fit Minors with whitewall tyres at extra cost to suit prevailing fashions. US dealers also added locally-manufactured Amco overrider bars to both front and rear bumpers to give the Minors a degree of protection against the American habit of parking by feel rather than by eye.

Overseas assembly of cars from CKD kits continued at a high level, too. In the Irish Republic, India, Holland, South Africa, Australia and New Zealand, assembly operations produced Minors with varying degrees of local content during the later Fifties and early Sixties. Some of these inevitably differed from the factory standard in areas such as paint, upholstery, tyres and electrical equipment.

Last but not least, we mustn't forget the special version of the Minor which was built during this period for disabled drivers. This was introduced shortly after the Minor 1000 itself, and was essentially a throwback to the Series II model, complete with 803cc engine and wide-ratio gearbox. Quite why disabled drivers would have wished for a less powerful car than the standard item has to be a matter for conjecture, although a cynic might suggest that BMC found this a convenient way of moving surplus stocks of the old engines and gearboxes!

All the Disabled Drivers' Minors were two-door models, and they were equipped with specially adapted drivers' seats on extended runners which were designed to allow easier access to the car. Some were also fitted at Cowley with hand controls. As the cars were clearly not Minor 1000s, even though they were made during the Minor 1000 period, they reverted to Series II badging as simple Morris Minors.

CHAPTER 5

The later Minor 1000s

1,098cc models, 1962-1971

After the formation of BMC, the Morris Minor was no longer developed in isolation. Items such as interior trim and suspension were unique to the car, and these did follow their own path; but where components could be shared with other BMC models – engines and gearboxes, for example – the Minor's development was always guided by the corporate plan. That much had become evident in 1952, when the 803cc engine also used in the Austin A30 had turned the Series MM into a Series II. Much the same had happened again in 1956 when the 948cc engine and associated new gearbox had been developed to suit both the Austin A35 and the Minor 1000. BMC performed the trick a third time in 1962, when they announced a new engine size for a whole range of models of which the Minor was just one.

What had happened this time was that the arrival of the new Austin and Morris 1100 front-wheel-drive cars had prompted a decision to reduce the number of different versions of the A-series engine in production. From now on there would be three sizes and four configurations. These would be 848cc for transverse installation in the Mini, 997cc for transverse installation in the Mini-Cooper, and 1,098cc for either transverse or conventional installation in all other small cars and light commercials. Thus the new 1100 models had transverse editions of the engine, while conventional versions went into the Austin A40, the A35 van (the saloons had been dropped), the Austin-Healey Sprite, the MG Midget ..... and of course the Morris Minor.

So while the 30% power increase (to 48bhp) which the 1,098cc engine brought to the Minor was more than welcome, it would be wrong to imagine that the new engine had been specifically engineered for the car. It had, of course, been heavily redeveloped, with both bigger bores and a longer stroke, a crankcase which was both strengthened and ribbed, and a tougher crankshaft. The Minor's gearbox, shared of course with other BMC models, had also been redeveloped to cope with this power increase. Its ribbed casing added strength, while for the driver the most welcome new feature was baulk-ring synchromesh instead of the cone-type, which was only too easy to beat with a fast change.

Not only had the gearbox been beefed-up to cope with the more powerful engine; a bigger 7¼-inch clutch replaced the 6¼-inch type, thus reducing the chance of clutch judder from the additional torque. However, if the clutch could be persuaded to bite hard, the 1,098cc Minor revealed axle tramp worse than that which had occasioned comment on the 948cc models! The fatter tyres (5.20 x 14s instead of the 5.00 x 14 size standard since 1948) might have been a contributory factor here, of course.

BMC also gave the 1,098cc Minors bigger 8-inch front brakes in place of the earlier 7-inch drums, and reduced the internal diameters of the master cylinder and rear wheel cylinders to make the braking system the best on any variety of Minor. They raised the final-drive gearing from 4.55:1 to 4.22:1 as well, reasoning that the taller ratio would give more relaxed cruising and aid fuel economy. That explains

This 1951 two-door saloon, see Chapter 2, was pictured by Tony Aston for *Minor Monthly* magazine. Note the wheels, painted in Ivory to contrast with the Black body. By this time, stocks of the original 'split' bumpers had been exhausted, and a full-size, fully-chromed item was in use.

This splendid 1955 four-door Series II was the winner of Minorex '95 and was pictured for *Minor Monthly* magazine by Robert Hawkins. Chapter 3 tells the Series II story.

An idyllic setting was chosen for this 1965 BMC publicity picture of a Minor 1000 four-door saloon – by this time with the enlarged 1,098cc engine. Note also the large front indicator/sidelamp clusters, which came in with the model.

why the 1,098cc Minor was not really capable of higher speeds than the 948cc model which it replaced. The older 4.55:1 axle remained available to special order and, of course, increased acceleration at the expense of top speed, cruising refinement and fuel economy. Refinement certainly was an issue with the lower axle gearing, too, because the 1,098cc engine could be quite noisy at high revs.

The new Minor should really perhaps have been renamed, and the obvious thing for BMC to do was to rename it a Minor 1100. That they didn't do so was probably because they were afraid that the public might confuse it with the new front-wheel-drive Morris 1100. So the 1,098cc Minor remained a Minor 1000, or a Minor Series V in-house. It didn't take the Series IV designation which would have followed logically from the Series III designation applied to the 948cc cars, because that had been inexplicably allocated to the Mini-Minor in 1959! The new engine, gearbox, brakes and tyres weren't the only things which distinguished the Series V car from the original 948cc Minor 1000, of course – and more of those other differences in a minute –

but they did contribute more than their fair share to the continuing sales success of the Minor.

Even so, the Minor was well past its prime. Sales had started to decline after their 1958 peak, and by 1961 it was already clear that the Minor's days must be numbered. Even the introduction of the re-engined Minor 1000 didn't stop the sales slide, and over the next nine years Minor sales gradually dropped away until they had reached a level where BMC could no longer justify keeping in production what was by then a 22-year-old design. Yet the car still had its devotees, and *Motoring Life* magazine perceptively revealed who they were in a 1969 issue. "For the type of man who doesn't know anything about motoring but knows exactly what he wants, the Morris 1000 is one of the rare cars that can give it him. Here is the most completely disinfested thing on wheels, with not a living bug left after all those twenty-one years in production. A car that can give such unfalteringly trouble-free service can no longer be said to have faults; they are now merely characteristic foibles, like panama hats or walrus moustaches, and very nearly as revered." To Minor enthusiasts today, those words may sound none too flattering, but the fact was that every one of them was true.

The Minor had already become a living legend, and for very good reasons, as *Motoring Life* went on to say. "The Minor has let the world of fashion pass it serenely by ... Looking dowdy, fat and 'fortyish may not matter; but there would be no scope on the roads of the 'seventies for a car with the performance standards of the 'forties, and this is where the Minor scores ..... even over the VW." Finally, "There isn't a safer car on the road (ask any insurance man); or an easier one to break into (via the boot); or a more considerate one on tyres (ask Dunlop)."

The Minor actually went on to outlive not only Morris Motors who had conceived it but also BMC which had been formed when Morris merged with Austin. By the time the last Minor was built in 1971, BMC had been swallowed up into British Leyland, and it may well have been BL's need to rationalize its products (a need even more urgent than BMC's had been 16 years earlier) which proved to be the final nail in the Minor's coffin. The timetable fits: in 1968, BMC became part of BL; in June 1969 the last Minor Convertible was built; in November 1970 the last Minor saloon was built; and in April 1971 came the final Traveller. That same month, BL announced the Morris Marina, deliberately conceived as a simple car and intended to replace the Minor. The Marina, however, was widely criticized and never captured the Minor's market.

Changes: from 1962 to 1971

The first 1,098cc Minors were built at Cowley in September 1962, and the car was introduced to the buying public at the Earls Court Motor Show in October. For the moment, the new engine, gearbox, brakes and axle gearing really were the only improvements: even the paint colours hadn't been changed from the last of the 948cc Minors, although the unpopular Highway Yellow was no longer listed. Our car-spotting schoolboys had to look very carefully indeed to tell one of these early 1,098cc cars from a 948cc model, and probably the only way they could do so

Clearly visible in this side view of a 1,098cc Minor 1000 is the revised upper B-pillar, with an extruded pressing where the semaphore trafficator had been on earlier models.

The convertible also appeared in Series II guise, complete with rigidly-mounted side window frames. In this rear view, note how the convertible top sits proud of the bodywork. This car is a 1954 example as featured in Chapter 3, although the rear lamp clusters and door mirror are a more modern addition.

A smart Black, Ivory and Red colour scheme. This 1966 Minor 1000 two-door was photographed by Jon Betts for *Minor Monthly* magazine.

The 1,098cc engine is seen to good advantage in the engine bay of this well-preserved Minor 1000 Convertible.

was by checking the tyre size stamped into the rubber or by looking inside to see if the handbrake was the new type with a white plastic release button!

BMC eked out the changes over the next few years, probably reasoning that a large package of changes introduced all at once would not give a significant boost to sales but that small changes introduced at regular intervals would at least help to keep sales alive. So for the 1964 models announced in October 1963, there were a redesigned windscreen washer system and – at last! – a keylock in the doors on both sides of the car! Also new were a zonc-toughened windscreen, a new wiper system with the arms operating in parallel and longer wiper blades, and new lamps at front and rear. These were much bigger than before. The front ones had a large round lens divided horizontally into clear and amber sections, while the rear ones also incorporated an amber section; in both cases, these were for the turn signals. There was also a mid-season change on the home market, when BMC dealers began to fit a pair of static seat belts to every new Minor they sold. This was in anticipation of the following year's legislation

Conventional windscreen wipers which operated in parallel were fitted by the time this two-door Minor was built in 1966. Its owner's membership of the Morris Minor Owners' Club is evident from the badge on the grille.

A year after production of the 1,098cc Minor had started, the rear lamp units were switched to the enlarged items seen here, which carried both the stop/tail and indicator lights.

that all new cars must have seat belts. Inertia-reel belts could be fitted as an extra-cost option, but rarely were.

The 1965-model Minors at the October 1964 Motor Show advertised that season's heavily-revised interior. Seats and door trims lost their stitching and were instead 'panelled' in cheaper heat-formed vinyl (which in later years proved impossible to repair satisfactorily). The central speedometer now had a black face, and was backed by an anodized trim panel which was flanked by vertical chrome finisher strips. It also carried a new warning light which advised of a blockage in the oil filter – a rather useless piece of gimmickry which was abandoned at the end of 1969. A two-spoke steering wheel similar to that on the Minis and 1100s replaced the three-spoke type, and the passenger glovebox was given a lid – again!

Then came a few concessions to crash safety, which was

Sunshine and the countryside bring out the best in a well-preserved Minor 1000 convertible like this 1969 model.

Robert Hawkins' picture of a late-model Traveller shows the characteristic wooden body frame and the rear light arrangement.

Tony Aston's picture, used by courtesy of *Minor Monthly* magazine, shows a 1967 four-door Minor 1000. Finished in Old English White, the car has its wheels and grille finished to match.

gradually attracting the attention of British motor manufacturers towards the middle of the Sixties. The sun visors on 1965-model Minors were made of crushable material and the interior mirror was given a plastic edge, while a black crash-pad on the front edge of the parcels shelf was supposed to give some protection to the front passengers' knees in a collision. Probably of greater benefit was the combined ignition and starter switch, which meant that drivers no longer had to press a separate button to operate the starter after inserting the ignition key. Similarly, most buyers must have thought the new automatic bootlid support strut was more useful than a bit of flimsy crash-padding!

For 1966, there were no changes. The 1967 model-year brought nothing more than sealed-beam headlamps, and the 1968 Minors were distinguished mainly by new colours. Old English White disappeared from the range, and so grilles were now painted in the new Snowberry White and

wheels in Dark Silver. The following year was similarly fallow, and the only thing which 1970 brought of any note was the option of fully-reclining front seats. These remained pretty rare, and were, of course, available only on saloons and Travellers, as the Convertibles had already ceased production.

British Leyland was keen to clear the Cowley works for some new assembly lines. The Convertible went out of production in June 1969 and Traveller assembly was moved to Adderley Park, Birmingham, the following month, where it joined the light commercial versions of the Minor which were already being built there. New colour schemes accompanied this move, although the saloons remained available in the colours introduced for the 1968 season. At Cowley, Minor assembly was now restricted to saloons, and BL shut down their production lines in November 1970, the last example being built on the 12th of the month.

The final changes, then, were made only to the Travellers, which remained available for the 1971 model-year. New colour-schemes were introduced in June 1970, and from January 1971 some Travellers had the steering column locks which had been fitted to a few earlier export cars. At the same time, static front seat belts were fitted on the assembly lines, to meet new seat-belt legislation which became effective on January 1.

Was the last Minor of all celebrated in the sort of ceremony such a well-liked model deserved? Sadly, it wasn't. The last saloon was fêted as it came off the assembly lines in November 1970, but the last Traveller was granted no such honour. Even that was not the last Minor of all, which was actually a GPO van version built in December 1971. The Adderley Park plant was, of course, an assembly plant primarily for commercial vehicles, and commercial vehicles were simply not treated like that.

It was an attitude which would unfortunately become all too typical of British Leyland as its corporate thrashings bankrupted what remained of the British car industry in the

The revised horn push with its large 'M' motif had arrived on the 948cc cars.

Pressed fibreboard door trims were characteristic of the 1,098cc Minors.

Andy is not only a florist but also a Minor fan! This 1971 pick-up is an Austin-badged variant and is still in everyday use for its owner's business in Accrington, Lancashire.

first half of the Seventies. In due course, when the Adderley Park plant was closed down, even some of the records relating to the production of Minor Travellers were lost. The British Motor Industry Heritage Trust has done its best with the surviving documents, and it thinks that 1,619,958 Minors of all kinds were built. One day, though, some records might be discovered in a dusty cupboard which will prove that figure to be incorrect ...

Minors in the USA
The Minor was still sold in the USA in 1,098cc form, but sales were declining in that market as rapidly as sales elsewhere. A laminated windscreen was standard on US models, which also had all-red rear light lenses and all-clear lenses on the front sidelight-and-indicator units. What finally killed the Minor in the USA, though, was the introduction of exhaust emissions regulations. Morris made

By the time this 1970-season British Leyland publicity picture was taken, the Convertible had ceased production. The days of the Traveller and the saloons – seen here in four-door guise – were already numbered.

The open road and a Minor 1000 Convertible ... this white car is one of the last made, and was not registered until 1971.

a gesture in the right direction with positive crankcase ventilation through a breather control valve, but it quickly became apparent that the car could not be made to meet the 1968 Federal regulations without expensive major work which would have left it wheezing and arthritic. That work was therefore never done, and the Minor slipped almost unnoticed off the list of cars available in the USA.

Police Minors and Panda cars
In Britain, the trend during the Sixties was to give

66

Dashboard of a late Minor 1000 Convertible. Note that there was only one glovebox lid by this stage, an open compartment being provided in front of the driver.

The inviting interior of a Minor 1000 Convertible on a hot summer's day. Just under 75,000 open-top Minors of various types were produced from 1948 to 1969.

An interesting series of messages about the Minor Traveller were conveyed by this 1965 BMC publicity shot – but it made a nice picture, anyway.

These large rear lights arrived in 1963. The locking fuel filler cap was an aftermarket accessory.

Period piece: the supplying dealer's decal on the glovebox lid of a late Sixties 1,098cc Traveller.

Policemen larger 'beat' areas to cover. As a result, the familiar bobby on foot or on his bicycle gradually disappeared, to be replaced by the Constable on a moped or in a small car. The Minor 1000 proved to be ideal for this kind of work, and sizeable numbers were taken on by Police forces all over Britain.

Although some Police Minors were painted white or blue all over, the majority were probably painted in the two-tone livery of the Panda car (a name inspired by the two-tone appearance of the animal!). These were two-door saloons, finished in Bermuda Blue with Police White doors which carried 'POLICE' identification. There was also an illuminated Police sign on the roof, and a special zipped headlining allowed access to the wiring associated with this, while a Lucas 11AC alternator was usually fitted to deal with the extra electrical demands. Somehow, the image of the local bobby in his Panda car was almost as comforting as the sight of him wheeling his bicycle along country lanes, a fact which spoke volumes for the cosy image associated with the Minor at this period as well!

The front face of a family favourite. This immaculate example was photgraphed in the mid-Nineties at the Bromley Pageant of Motoring, where dozens of Minors can usually be found amongst the massive turnout of cars. Over 1.6 million Minors in various forms were produced between 1948 and 1971.

Pictured here with several after-market accessories adorning it is one of the 350 celebration Minor Million models produced in the early Sixties; all of them were painted in Lilac with an off-white interior.

CHAPTER 6

Light Commercials

Vans, pick-ups and chassis-cabs, 1953-1971

When the Morris Minor arrived in 1948 to replace the Morris Eight, there wasn't much doubt that the old Morris Z 5cwt van based on the Eight would disappear before too long. At Cowley, there wasn't much hesitation in deciding to make a new 5cwt van out of the Minor, either, although it would be 1953 before the first light commercial derivatives of the Minor went on sale. In the meantime, the old Z van stayed in production.

Designing its replacement wasn't too high on the Morris priorities list, and so the Minor had been on sale for nearly two years before the first prototype light commercial was built under Cowley project number DO 954 in June 1950. It was a van, painted green and bearing the identification number EX/SMV/174. A second followed in February 1951, this one painted blue and bearing the number EX/SMM/178. Also built at this time was EX/SMM/179, which might possibly have been a prototype pick-up. Then in November 1951 came EX/SMM/195, described in existing records as a 'flat floor chassis' and actually a chassis/cab unit (project DO 1222) for special bodywork. This last prototype was bodied as a fire tender and served with the Morris Motors Fire Brigade for several years. It is now preserved in the Heritage Museum at Gaydon.

So by the end of 1951, Morris had built prototypes of the three light commercial variants they intended to put into series production – the van, the pick-up and the chassis/cab. All the prototypes at this stage had side-valve engines, of course, although by the time the commercials went into production in 1953 the overhead-valve 803cc engine had taken over and there were no 'production' side-valve models.

Structure

It simply wasn't possible to hack away the rear half of a Minor saloon and build a van body on the floorpan which remained: so much of the monocoque's strength lay in the body that an alternative solution had to be found. What Morris Motors actually did was to take the four-door Minor saloon structure from the central door pillars forward, and weld a rigid box-section chassis frame to the back of it. The rear chassis side-members picked up on the rear of the integral strengthening rails which ran from the engine bay under the front floorpan, and arched up over the rear axle. The standard semi-elliptic springs were used at the back, although telescopic dampers replaced the saloons' lever-arm type from the beginning.

Onto this was built a van body, which stood taller than the front 'cab' section. It had twin rear doors, each with a small window, and panels were pressed into the upper body sides to create a framework for the signwriting which was then a feature of small vans. A swage line in the lower body sides helped to link the van back into the lines of the standard saloon doors and wings, but not all the front panels were taken from the saloon. For some reason, the van (and all other Minor commercials) had a bonnet without the raised moulding where saloons had their painted coachlines. The commercials also had a shorter edition of the front bumper, which wrapped around less

The Morris Minor van was always a neat-looking vehicle, as this picture of a Series II variant makes clear. Note how the front bumper does not wrap right around its support panel, but finishes short.

than the saloon type and left the ends of its mounting plinth exposed. As for a rear bumper, there was nothing more than a pair of rubber buffers.

The vans, of course, had an open cab back so that the driver could easily reach into the load area behind him. However, the pick-up models had an additional panel which closed off the back of the cab, and this panel could also be fitted to the chassis-cab Minors. (It wasn't fitted to those sent to Denmark for conversion into vans by the importers, DOMI, however.) The pick-up bed itself generally followed the lines of the van's lower body, but it had a drop-down tailgate instead of rear doors and carried

provision for mounting four steel hoops. These came with the optional canvas tilt which covered the whole of the pick-up bed and could be held by rope to cleats which were welded to the body sides if this option was specified. It's interesting that the Minor pick-up was a new departure for Morris, who had not built any pick-ups before but quickly recognized how useful such a vehicle might be to small tradesmen, builders, and so on.

Development

Over the 18 years of their production, the light commercials generally followed the same development pattern as the

Minor saloons. So there were 803cc Series II variants between 1953 and 1956, 948cc Series III variants between 1956 and 1962, and 1,098cc Series V variants thereafter (the Series IV designation was once again not allocated to any version of the Minor). In addition, from 1968 there were Austin-badged versions of the Series V, which were known as Series C types but which differed only cosmetically. All Minor commercials built up to 1962 had a 5cwt payload rating. Thereafter they were rated as 6cwt vehicles, and from 1968 the payload was raised to 8cwt.

Series II (803cc) variants differed from their equivalent saloons in subtle ways. They had no chromed insert in their windscreen rubbers, and their windscreen centre pillars and door window frames were painted in the body colour. Bumper blades and wiper arms were also painted silver instead of chromed, to save costs. All the Series II commercials had an exterior mirror bolted to the windscreen pillar on the driver's side, and the very first ones had fixed quarter-light windows in their doors as well. Interior trim was pretty Spartan, with black rubber mats

instead of carpets, and this aspect of the commercials at least didn't change throughout the production run. Seats were universally upholstered in brown Vynide, and Series II commercials built before February 1955 also had a painted wooden dashboard.

Changes certainly took their time to arrive, which is a good indication that the customers for the early Minor commercials were a satisfied bunch! Nothing changed (except in line with the saloons) until the 948cc engine replaced the 803cc type in 1956 to give Series III models, and then the next item of interest was a change to wing mirrors in place of the pillar-mounted rear-view mirror. It was another three years before any further changes were made. Even then, it was only that the optional passenger seat was given a folding back to make access to the rear of vans easier from the pavement! September 1962 saw the change to Series V models, which, of course, brought not only the 1,098cc engine but also larger windows in the rear doors of vans. As the engine had greater lugging power, Morris uprated the payload from 5cwt to 6cwt, but not

BMC did consider the idea of a van conversion with windows, but the extra tax payable on such vehicles in Britain appears to have put paid to the idea. The position of the sidelamps and the grille type make clear that the base vehicle was a Series MM, so this may have started life as one of the Minor LCV prototypes.

This delightful 1963 van is not quite what it seems, although the exterior looks standard: it has actually been subtly modified with uprated brakes, engine and gearbox. Its owner rebuilt it to resemble a 1/43 scale Corgi model of a Minor van finished in Castrol's distinctive livery. This picture was taken by Robert Hawkins for *Minor Monthly* magazine.

After 1968, the LCVs were available with Austin badges, and soon acquired the distinctive 'crinkly' Austin grille as well. This 1971 model is one of the last, and was pictured for *Minor Monthly* magazine by Tony Aston.

without fitting stiffer rear springs – now with eight leaves – to take the strain.

Keeping the Minor commercials competitive, Morris upgraded them further in 1968. The Series V models could handle an 8cwt payload (60% more than the original 1953 models), thanks once again to tougher suspension. This time, Morris fitted rear springs with seven thicker leaves, and strengthened the front suspension uprights, the steering levers and the torsion bars. On top of that, they fitted wider wheels with 4½J rims so that the Series V Minors (and the Series C Austins) could wear wider 5.60 x 14 tyres. These last versions of the commercial models also had black upholstery and separate indicator lights at the rear, which provoked a small change to the pressing of the rear lower panels. They also usually had wing mirrors mounted on a spring-loaded base.

Austin versions weren't all 8cwt types, because the first ones built in 1968 were to the older 6cwt specification. Austin vans, however, had a plastic Austin badge on their bonnets, plain hubcaps, and 'crinkly' grille bars to give

The pick-up's optional canvas tilt had the same design throughout LCV production, but there was only a single rear lamp before 1962 brought separate indicators and stop/tail lights.

A wide tailgate with a low loading height made the Minor pick-up very easy to use.

them at least some semblance of the Austin tradition. They also carried an Austin badge on the horn push in the centre of their steering wheels and an Austin badge on their engine rocker covers. For all that, nobody except an Austin salesman has ever called them anything except Austin-badged Minor commercials!

The honour of being the very last Minor of all actually went to a van, vehicle number M-AG5-327369, which was completed in December 1971. It was at least fitting that the van should have been delivered to the Post Office for mail delivery duties and was painted in the characteristic red livery which was seen on so many Minor vans in the Fifties, Sixties and early Seventies.

Vans for the GPO

It seems pretty certain that the main reason why Morris developed a van version of the Minor in the first place was to secure fleet orders from the GPO (General Post Office, which was then responsible for both mail and telephone services). The Morris Z van had fitted the GPO's needs

This Royal Mail van is one of the first examples to be delivered in 1953. Note the rubber front wings with headlamps perched on top, and the opening windscreen, which made roof-mounted wipers necessary.

admirably, and Morris could foresee regular orders for large batches if they could come up with a replacement which would suit the GPO as well. So once basic prototype testing had been done, a van was mocked-up for GPO representatives to inspect during January 1953, a few months in advance of the vehicle's public launch date. The GPO liked what they saw, and over the next 18 years took an estimated 50,000 Minor vans. They became a well-loved feature of the British street scene, and some of them remained in service until the end of the Seventies.

Even though the GPO vans had a number of common features, there were also several different types. Even the livery changed in later years. Mail vans were always painted pillar-box red, but the vans used by the GPO Engineers (essentially, those who worked on the telephones side of the business) were painted a rather drab olive green up to 1968. From that date on, the telephone engineers' vans were painted yellow, to match the new corporate colours of the Post Office Telephones division. Some of the earlier 'green' vans were definitely repainted yellow to match the latest deliveries, and in the early Seventies it was not uncommon to see a rather battered Post Office Telephones van showing traces of its original olive green paint under the yellow!

The very first Series II GPO vans had a specification which was all their own and which Morris had developed specially for this major fleet user. The most unusual feature was that the front wings were not made of metal but rather of unpainted black rubber. This was intended to reduce the

One of the GPO's 1958 deliveries – outwardly a 948cc type, but actually fitted with the older 803cc engine. The special Yale lock is visible on the driver's door, and the roof carries the 'pig's ear' indicator lamps characteristic of the period. By this stage, the rubber wings and opening windscreen had disappeared from the specification.

This early PO Telephones van shows its differences from the Royal Mail version by the addition of the roof-mounted ladder retaining rack and the lack of a security bar across the rear doors, although there was a hasp for fastening with a padlock to give extra security over and above the normal locking handle. The white lettering above the wheelarches are the tyre pressures.

By 1969 the Post Office Telephones vans had the new yellow livery and the larger rear windows without the mesh screens behind them, and the indicator flashers were now above the rear lights. The vehicles were supplied with brackets on the body sides to take an advertisement board but without hubcaps as this picture shows. (*All pictures of Royal Mail and Post Office Telephone vans are used by courtesy of the Post Office Archives.*)

costs associated with repairing minor body damage, but it must have brought other disadvantages with it because the rubber wings were discontinued in October 1954, after just over a year in production. The wings didn't incorporate headlamp housings, but instead carried free-standing headlamps which gave these early GPO vans a characteristic 'frog's-eye' appearance.

Early vans also came without a heater, because the GPO wasn't prepared to pay the extra for one of these (which was an option on the standard Minor commercials as well). However, they were prepared to put Morris to the trouble of redesigning the windscreen and wiper arrangements to compensate! So the split-screen Minor GPO vans always had the driver's sidescreen hinged from the top so that it

could be opened for improved visibility in poor conditions – a wonderfully archaic feature which didn't make the lives of GPO employees any more comfortable! It wasn't possible to find a foolproof way of using the standard wipers with this opening screen, and so the wipers on GPO vans were relocated above the windscreen on both sides.

Both the mail and telephone vans always had an inspection trap in the rear floor, and special towing and lifting brackets at the back. They also had wire mesh attached inside the windows of the two rear doors as a theft deterrent, and they had a wood-framed partition covered with wire mesh located between the driver and the van body, again for security reasons. On the mail vans, this covered only half the width of the van, but on telephone

This interior picture of a pick-up shows the support hoops for the optional canvas top.

A rubber seal was used between the cab and the back body of Minor vans.

vans it was full-width and also carried the spare wheel. Mail vans never had a passenger's seat, but usually carried a wicker basket in the space alongside the driver, where he could place letters and parcels without fear that they would slide about on the floor. The telephone engineers' van had a ladder-rack mounted on its roof, but the mail van didn't, while the mail van had an exterior locking bar across its rear doors and the telephone van didn't. Interiors were also fitted out differently, the engineers' van usually having a row of bins down either side of the van body while the mail van had no such fittings.

When the 948cc Minor was introduced in 1956, the GPO was happy to accept many of its new features, most notably the single-piece windscreen, which prompted the demise of the opening driver's sidescreen. Nevertheless, the GPO clearly sucked its collective teeth over the new and larger engine. Presumably reasoning that larger capacity meant larger fuel bills, the GPO therefore insisted on retaining the original 803cc engine – and Morris were happy to comply until 1964, when the GPO finally accepted that the latest

The optional canvas top was held in place by rope lashed through cleats on the sides of the pick-up body.

1,098cc engine wasn't such a bad idea after all! It was at the same time, incidentally, that the 803cc engine was discontinued for the Disabled Driver's Minor saloon, so perhaps Morris Motors had applied just a little bit of pressure on the GPO to accept the larger engines ...

Meanwhile, there had been some other changes. Lucas 'pig's-ear' flashing indicators were fitted on the outer edges of the van roof of the final Series II and on Series III models built before 1962. From 1957, both cab doors also sprouted massive Yale locks located just ahead of the drop-glass' leading edge. These were one result of a GPO crackdown on security, and were intended to ensure that careless van drivers did not leave their vans unlocked and vulnerable to theft. The Yale locks were, of course, self-locking, and so all

the driver had to remember to do was to take his key with him. The locking mechanism, it's interesting to know, was actually designed by Reg Job of the original Minor design team.

Then from 1962, the GPO decided to save even more money by taking their Minor vans without hubcaps. Both mail vans and telephone vans delivered from about 1964 had four clips on either side of the van body, where advertisement boards could be mounted. From 1969, the telephone vans also had a different type of ladder rack, made of aluminium instead of steel, and from about this time the wire mesh partition also disappeared from the inside.

The final order from the Post Office was for 2,350 mail vans, and these were delivered in 1971.

CHAPTER 7

Relatives at home and abroad

Riley, Wolseley and Australian derivatives

The Morris Minor had not been in production for more than a couple of years before the Nuffield Organisation began to think about its eventual replacement. It must have been during 1951 that Gerald Palmer, Group Chief Designer based at Cowley, started looking at a new Minor under the project code of DO 1058. Not much seems to have happened before the merger with Austin in 1952 led to a revitalized Minor with the A30's overhead-valve engine, and the project for a completely new Minor was probably shelved.

However, Len Lord returned to the charge some time in the mid-Fifties. Gerald Palmer had by then left BMC for Vauxhall Motors, and Lord asked Dick Burzi, the chief stylist at Austin's Longbridge plant, to have another look at the plans for a new Minor. Burzi drew up his own version of the DO 1058 car, and a single prototype (EX/266) was built, probably towards the end of 1955. This was fitted with the 1,200cc version of BMC's B-series engine which had first seen the light of day in 1954's Austin A40 Cambridge. There were probably a couple more prototypes built, as well: records suggest that EX/274 and EX/304 were also Morris 1200 versions of DO 1058.

What put paid to the Morris 1200 was the Suez crisis of 1956-57. When Egypt's President Nasser nationalized the Suez Canal, he forced oil tankers on their way to Europe to pay heavy taxes or take the long way round, and the result was a petrol shortage followed by rationing in Britain. The crisis was eventually resolved, but in the meantime sales of small cars which used little petrol shot up and those of thirsty larger-engined cars nose-dived. Morris Minor sales benefited, and all the reasons for introducing a bigger and thirstier Minor 1200 evaporated overnight.

However, Len Lord was not about to throw away the time and money which had gone into the DO 1058 project. He knew that some of BMC's overseas markets – and Australia in particular – wanted more power and performance, even from the small cars. So he instructed engineering chief Charlie Griffin to try the bigger-bore 1,489cc B-series engine in the Morris 1200, and to match it to a taller final drive ratio. Griffin did so, presumably modifying one of the existing Morris 1200 prototypes, and the result appears to have satisfied Lord. In fact, it pleased him so much that he decided the 1,500cc DO 1058 should not be handed over to BMC's Australian subsidiary lock, stock and barrel, but should also become the basis of a more expensive Minor derivative in Britain. So the car which had started out as a Minor replacement eventually went into production (in modified form) alongside the model it had been intended to replace.

BMC never intended to call the new British car a Minor, of course. There was more money to be made from producing non-identical-twin derivatives wearing the upmarket badges of Riley and Wolseley. A precedent for this had already been established: the existing Riley Pathfinder and Wolseley Six-Ninety were both derived from the same design, and similarly the Wolseley 4/44 and MG Magnette were essentially the same car behind the badging and trim. This kind of badge-engineering had been

The car which started it all was the Morris 1200. The original was drawn up by Gerald Palmer, but this is one of the later proposals styled by Dick Burzi. The registration number on this apparently roadworthy prototype would suggest that it was put on the road late in 1955 or early in 1956.

practised in the USA for many years, and BMC had quickly appreciated its cost-saving benefits – although it caused die-hard marque enthusiasts to foam at the mouth in the Fifties.

So DO 1058 appeared first in April 1957 as a Wolseley 1500 to capture the market for a well-appointed small car to appeal to older buyers, and was then announced in November that year as a Riley One-Point-Five with a more powerful engine and more fashionable colour schemes to appeal to those who wanted a small car which was fast and stylish. Both cars were well-received, and the Riley went on to outsell every earlier model to bear the Riley name while the Wolseley outsold every previous Wolseley. Between them, they greatly enhanced the reputation of the car which lay at the heart of both – Alec Issigonis' Morris Minor.

The Wolseley 1500
Despite the Austin-styled body with its characteristic rolled-

over rocker panels below the doors, despite a BMC B-series engine with 50% more capacity than the contemporary Minor's A-series, and despite the badges and different pretensions which went with them, both the Wolseley 1500 and the Riley One-Point-Five were Morris Minors underneath. This was quite literally true, in fact, as their bodies were built on the floorpan of the Minor and used its entire suspension and steering gear. Axle ratios were different, however, and a taller 3.73:1 replaced the Minor's 4.22:1 to allow relaxed cruising and good fuel economy with the bigger engines.

The Wolseley's single-carburettor engine put out 50bhp and gave the car a maximum speed of around 80mph, while fuel economy was still good at around 35mpg. The outside was discreet, as befitted the Wolseley marque, with single-tone or restrained two-tone paint schemes and the traditional illuminated badge on the radiator grille. The car also bore a winged-W mascot on the leading edge of its

The first of the DO 1058 cars to enter production was the Wolseley 1500, seen here in a 1957 BMC publicity picture.

The Mk II versions of the Wolseley 1500 differed very little from the original 1957 model, but the facelifted Mk III of 1961 brought this larger grille and modified chrome-work on the front wings.

The two-tone colour scheme and whitewall tyres seen in this publicity shot of a 1961 Mk III Wolseley 1500 somehow seem too racy for the car; its sober nature was better suited to monotone colours and less garish accessories.

bonnet, and became the last Wolseley to do so because some European countries declared such protrusions dangerous to pedestrians and banned them in the mid-Sixties. Inside were wood and leather, again as expected of the marque, and the walnut veneer dashboard had neatly symmetrical styling with a large loudspeaker for the radio in its centre.

From the beginning of production until the end, all the Wolseley 1500s came from the former Austin plant at Longbridge, although a number left there as kits of parts for CKD (Completely Knocked Down) assembly overseas. Notable among these were the cars destined for Australia between 1957 and 1959, and those intended for the Republic of Ireland during 1957. These latter, which were built in only small numbers, were not actually Wolseley 1500s at all but rather Wolseley 1200s, because they had the 1,200cc B-series engine originally planned for the Morris 1200 in 1956! Very little is known about them, but it seems probable that they would have had the engine in its 42bhp Austin A40 Cambridge state of tune, with torque of

58lb.ft. The slow-selling A40 was discontinued during 1957, and it took the 1,200cc B-series engine with it; BMC presumably decided that it was not worth keeping the engine in production for tiny numbers of CKD Wolseleys.

The Wolseley found a waiting market, and BMC quickly cashed in on its popularity by introducing a 'Fleet' version in January 1959. This made available all the cachet of the Wolseley name at a cheaper price, but in the process the trim had to be simplified and Vynide upholstery replaced the standard leather. Two-tone paint was also deleted from the options list. The standard car was unchanged but now became known as the Family model, and both models were given wider 5.60 x 16 tyres during May 1959.

It was a year after that when Mk II editions of the Wolseley 1500 appeared in the showrooms. They were recognizable from outside by different chrome trim on their front wings, and by the fact that the hinges for bonnet and bootlid were now hidden from view. On the inside, a parcels shelf had been added under the facia, but otherwise the cars remained as they had been since 1957.

As announced in 1957, the Riley One-Point-Five had a lot more chrome at its front end than the Morris Minor on which it was based. Look closely, and the family resemblance is clear, however. This is a late-1960 model, which was unchanged externally.

The Mk IIs lasted for just over two years, and were replaced by Mk III models in October 1961. This time, BMC had made more than simple cosmetic revisions, and the cars had an improved gearbox with stronger bearings, while they had been lowered on their suspension by an inch to improve handling. Interior changes centred on modified seats, which gave passengers more headroom and more legroom, but now came in monotone instead of the two-tone schemes of the earlier cars. Otherwise, the cars could be recognized by their new side grilles containing large round lamps which combined flashers and sidelamps, and by their larger rear lamps which had come from the Austin A40 Farina.

Not many changes were made subsequently. From October 1962 there was a new crankshaft; from the following January the engine compression ratio was raised from 7.2:1 to 8.3:1; and in November 1964 the interiors were fitted with crushable sun visors and plastic-framed mirrors in a small concession to improving crash safety. The last Wolseley 1500s were made in April 1965 and brought the total made of this Minor derivative up to 103,394, an average of about 12,900 cars for each year since its introduction.

The Riley One-Point-Five
The Riley version of the DO 1058 car never sold in anything like the numbers of its Wolseley sister, and just 39,568 were built between November 1957 and the end of production in April 1965. Average annual production was therefore in the region of 4,900 cars a year. Like the Wolseleys, the Rileys were built at Longbridge, although the first 150 cars were actually assembled at Abingdon, home of Rileys since 1948.

The Riley was more expensive than the Wolseley 1500, and this extra cost was largely justified by its more powerful engine. Once again a 1,489cc B-series type, it nevertheless had twin SU carburettors for a higher power output of 68bhp and a maximum speed of nearly 85mph. Fuel consumption was inevitably poorer, but even so returns of 28-30mpg were possible, which was quite reasonable for a

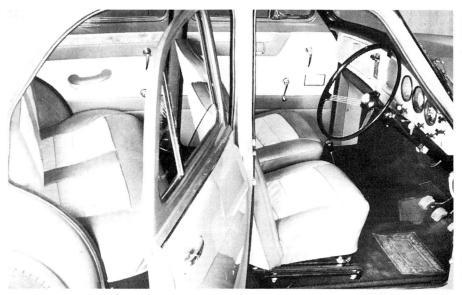

All the DO 1058 cars were four-door models, and both the trim and dashboard differed from their Morris Minor equivalents. This is the interior of an early Riley One-Point-Five.

The 1961 facelift which created the Mk II versions of the Riley One-Point-Five brought new side grilles and indicator/sidelamp units.

car of this type at the time.

Rileys also looked more sporting than the Wolseleys, invariably being delivered with two-tone paintwork in some eye-catching schemes which would have looked out of place on the more sober Wolseley. Rileys had more chrome, too, plus special wheeltrims and a different front panel, front bumper and grille. There was wood on the facia, but not on the doors, and the seats were upholstered in two-tone Vynide while the instruments (which included a rev-counter) were grouped directly ahead of the driver in a manner consistent with the Riley's sporting image.

Riley development generally echoed that of its sister Wolseley. Wider tyres were introduced in May 1959, and then Mk II models were announced in May 1960. These had concealed bonnet and bootlid hinges like the Mk II Wolseleys, together with a parcels shelf under the facia. The Mk IIIs introduced in October 1961 had the revised side grilles and combined sidelamp/indicator units, plus the Austin A40 rear lamps, improved monotone seats, stronger gearbox and lowered suspension. October 1962 brought the

same revised crankshaft, and November 1964 the same small concessions to crash safety in the interior.

It's interesting that BMC did contemplate an early-Sixties revamp of the DO 1058 design, and made a mock-up based on a Riley One-Point-Five which incorporated tailfins and lights like those on the bigger Farina-styled Riley 4/68. The design was known as the ADO27R (the R presumably being for Riley). Nothing came of it, however.

Australian relatives

When BMC decided to let its Australian subsidiary have a crack at selling the revamped Minor with its 1.5-litre engine, it was aiming to cater for a specific market niche down under. The Minor itself was already on sale there, and in fact there would be a celebratory press junket in July 1958 as the 50,000th Minor came off the assembly lines at BMC Australia's Victoria Park plant in Sydney. That figure makes BMC's position in Australia sound rather more rosy than it was, however.

In fact, the Australian derivatives of the revamped Minor would be introduced into a declining market. The Nuffield Organisation and Austin had both done very well in Australia during the late Forties, when American dollars were scarce and the country had naturally turned towards the centre of the Commonwealth for vehicles of all kinds. In those years, the two companies between them were supplying something like 30% of all new cars sold in Australia, and were jointly second only to the locally-made Holden. However, the honeymoon did not last. Sales dropped quite sharply in the early Fifties, and by 1952 the newly-amalgamated Nuffield and Austin could lay claim to only 19% of the market. Under BMC, that percentage dropped even further until by 1958 it had reached only 12%.

So BMC Australia needed something to revive its flagging fortunes. What it should have done, and failed to do, was to offer a big and rugged six-cylinder saloon like those which Australians were buying in ever greater numbers. Instead, the company decided to settle for a Morris Minor derivative which was in truth a small car made to look bigger by

The resemblance between the Australian-built Morris Major of 1958 and the Wolseley 1500 is obvious in this picture.

The instrument panel of the Morris Major was centrally-mounted, although the main dial had a distinctly Austin flavour. In the Austin Lancer, the panel was mounted directly ahead of the driver.

styling changes and made to go faster by a larger engine. It never sold well, and BMC Australia recognized its mistake early on; after just one year in production, it stretched the wheelbases of its new Minor-derived models by no fewer than 6 inches to give them greater appeal.

The first of the revamped Minors to go into production at Victoria Park was actually none other than the Wolseley 1500, which made its Australian debut in September 1957. This was simply the British car built in Australia, however, in just the same way as the contemporary Morris Minor. While the Wolseley helped Australians to get used to the new shape, a major building programme was under way to provide Victoria Park with a new body pressing shop and a manufacturing facility for engines, gearboxes and axles. This was opened in July 1958 at the same time as the 50,000th Minor came off the lines, and from now on BMC Australia was in a position to build its own special derivatives.

Two prototypes of these special derivatives were built in Britain under the project code of DO 1101, and were numbered as EX/321 and EX/322. It is not clear whether one was badged as an Austin and one as a Morris, but when DO 1101 entered production in Australia it had been badge-engineered in typical BMC fashion. One version was called an Austin Lancer while the other was called a Morris Major, and the pair of them were introduced alongside the Wolseley 1500. The Lancer had the Wolseley 1500 bodyshell with a slatted Austin grille all-too-obviously filling the cutout for the Wolseley original, while the Major had a plainer grille derived directly from the uninspired shape on Dick Burzi's Morris 1200 prototype. Both of them had an Austin A35-style combined instrument panel, fitted ahead of the driver on the Lancer and in the dash centre on the Major. There were other trim differences, but the engines in both were 1,489cc B-series types in the same state of tune as the Wolseley 1500.

The Lancer and Major lasted just one year in their original form. From July 1959, both they and the Wolseley 1500 were withdrawn from the Australian market. The Wolseley did not reappear, but the Lancer and the Major were heavily restyled and re-engineered to become Series II

An extra 6 inches in the wheelbase provided the main element in the Mk II Austin Lancer, although new front and rear designs were also added to make the car look different from the rather unsuccessful Mk I.

Tailfins were also added to the Mk II versions of the Austin Lancer and Morris Major. This Morris later found its way to the UK, where it was pictured by *Classic and Sportscar* magazine.

models. Their rear axles were moved backwards by 6 inches and their tails were restyled with longer rear overhangs bearing tailfins and new rear lights (though the design was quite unlike the ADO27R experiment). What this did for the passenger space was minimal, although it did put all the seats well within the wheelbase for a better ride. It also gave the cars a bigger boot, which must have been welcomed. As part of the Series II makeover, the

Lancer also lost its Wolseley-like grille to a more horizontal affair which generally made its front end look like the Ford Prefect 107E which was just about to enter production.

The Series II Lancer and Major lasted until 1962, and never did become the big sellers which BMC Australia had hoped. In April that year, the Lancer was replaced by the Austin A40 Farina, and the Major was re-engined with the 1,622cc B-series while its styling and interior were again revitalized. The result was called a Morris Major Elite and it lasted until 1964, when BMC Australia replaced it with the new front-wheel drive 1100 family.

A Riley One-Point-Five pictured on the Mobil Economy Run with its crew in attendance. The competition story of the Morris Minor and its relatives is told in the following chapter.

CHAPTER 8

Unlikely competitors

Minors, Rileys and Wolseleys in race and rally

Competition was not really relevant to the development of the Minor in the way that it was for so many other cars. Morris Motors, and later BMC, did provide a degree of support to a number of privateers who took Minors on international rallies and out onto the circuits, but there was never any very serious attempt to push the Minor as a competition car. Underpowered for most of its life, and heavy when compared to most of the competitive small saloons in the under-1,000cc and later the 1,000cc-1,500cc classes, the Minor would have needed some quite substantial development to turn it into a winner. Neither Morris nor BMC seems to have thought it was worth the effort; the car was selling more than well enough anyway, and competition success would probably not have made much difference.

Even so, the Minor most definitely did have a competition history, and as a result it is eligible nowadays for many of the 'nostalgia' events which attempt to recreate the motoring of the Fifties. It also did surprisingly well with surprisingly little development in the hands of the noted all-woman rally crew of Pat Moss and Ann Wisdom, and a number of privateers persevered with their Minors to good effect in the circuit racing of the British Saloon Car Championship in the later Fifties and early Sixties.

It was the arrival of the Mini which really put an end to the Minor's competition hopes, as BMC's support for and interest in small saloon car competition inevitably switched to the newer and infinitely more able car. The Mini was announced in 1959; the Minor's last appearance with full 'works' backing was in 1960. However, the Riley 1.5 had put in an appearance by this stage, and with its more powerful engine was a much more promising competitions car. It never achieved very much in the rally world, but between 1958 and 1964 there were a number of formidable and successful Rileys on the circuits in Britain. A few cars continued in action after that, but the arrival in their class of the all-conquering Ford Cortina GT during 1963, and the end of Riley production in 1965, signalled the end of the cars' prominence in competition.

Side-valve Minors
The ancient side-valve engine in the Series MM Minors could be tuned much more than many people today seem to think, although it took a lot of work to make a side-valve Minor competitive with its contemporaries propelled by overhead-valve engines. As the regulations governing the major competitive events were fairly strict about modifications, not a lot of side-valve Minors were heavily tuned. An exception to this general rule was Alan Foster's Series MM equipped with an overhead-valve Alta conversion and supported by the Alta concern. In the first half of the Fifties, it acquitted itself rather well in saloon car racing on British circuits.

The MM also put in an appearance in international rallies, and works-supported examples did run in the Monte Carlo rally. The first entry was made as early as 1949, when the all-woman crew of 'Bill' Wisdom, Betty Haig and Barbara

The Minor soon began to appear in international rallies, entered by privateers. This Series MM 'high-headlamp' model is pictured on the 1952 Monte Carlo event, in which it had clearly sustained some small damage. Note the electric screen demister on the driver's side - a popular aftermarket accessory of the time.

Marshall achieved a very creditable second place in the *Coupe des Dames*. However, this was fairly low-key stuff as far as the overall international rallying scene went and it would be wrong to get the idea that the Minor's participation in rallying during the early Fifties had any great significance.

The Minor 1000

The Series II Minor with its 803cc engine never did become a competition car. The engine offered little more performance than the older 918cc side-valve type, but the ill-chosen gearbox ratios were probably what put most people off using Series II Minors in competition. Besides, in the under-1,000cc classes, the same engine and gearbox were available in the rather lighter Austin A30, the car for which the gearbox and its ratios had been designed. BMC knew that as well as anybody else, and preferred to lend support to privateers using the Austin.

However, the Minor re-entered the frame of potential competition mounts as soon as the new 948cc Minor 1000 was announced in 1956. Not only was its engine larger and more powerful, but it also had a new gearbox with properly-matched ratios. This immediately gave it some appeal to privateers, and BMC themselves were not far behind in allowing their new Competitions Department to prepare a small number of Minor 1000s.

Probably the most famous works-prepared Morris Minor 1000 was registered as NMO 933 and was regularly driven by the BMC works team of Pat Moss and Ann Wisdom. Always better known as 'Granny' – for reasons which are all too obvious when the car is compared with some of the pair's other works mounts – NMO 933 made its first appearance in the Tulip rally in 1957. On that occasion, it was driven by BMC's works team leader, John Gott. The ladies Moss and Wisdom took it over for that year's Liège-Rome-Liège rally, when it bore them to second place in the *Coupe des Dames* and to a largely unexpected 23rd place overall, as well as beating the Austin A35s for the first time.

The Moss and Wisdom pairing took their Minor on the 1958 Monte, though they were forced to retire from this

Stretching the Minor's legs at Silverstone, in this instance during the MCC meeting in 1954. Convertibles were every bit as popular as saloons for competitive events, as this 1951 Series MM shows.

The Minor was very popular in club events such as this one at Silverstone in May 1954. The driver of this 'low-light' saloon was Alan Foster.

rally. Then for 1960, 'Granny' was entered for one last time in the RAC rally – which had new and tougher regulations that year – though without result.

'Granny' was by no means the only 948cc Minor to see competition in the late Fifties, of course, and nor was she the first. The earliest Minor 1000 prepared by the BMC works was one driven by the father and son team of Edward

Reversing tests were a feature of the gentlemanly small rallies of the Fifties. Here, a Convertible is put through its paces on the 1954 Plymouth Presidential rally.

particularly difficult event. Next came that year's RAC rally, when they managed a superb fourth place overall, and then later on the Viking rally, which earned them another second place in the *Coupe des Dames*. These results and others gained in different BMC works machines (among them the new Riley 1.5s) earned for the pair that year's Ladies' European Championship. 'Granny' entered several more events in 1959 – the Sestrière, the Circuit of Ireland, the RAC and the Morecambe rally – although it had rather less success. The best the Moss-Wisdom team could achieve was a fifth in class and the *Coupe des Dames* on the Sestrière

Scrutineering at Blackpool on the 1954 RAC rally, with Minors lined up for attention. The lead car – its Oxford registration suggesting factory ownership – was a brand-new Series II model.

Proving the car's and their own toughness, Pat Moss and Ann Wisdom took part in the gruelling 1957 Liège-Rome-Liège rally in this well-known Minor 1000, nicknamed 'Granny', and finished 23rd overall and runners-up for the *Coupe des Dames*.

'Granny' again, this time on the 1959 Circuit of Ireland rally, with Pat Moss and Ann Wisdom tackling Corkscrew Hill on their way to the Ladies' award, second in class and 14th overall.

and Ray Brookes in the 1957 Sestrière rally; in fact, it would probably have been entered in the Monte Carlo rally if that had not been cancelled because of the Suez Crisis and the petrol shortages which resulted in Europe. There was works support for the Minor in the Tulip rally that year, as well, as there would be in a number of later events.

However, BMC's interest in the Minor as a competitions machine was about to be overtaken by its interest in the Riley – and even Wolseley – 1½-litre derivatives. Once those two had reached the showrooms in 1958, there were different fish to fry.

Rileys and Wolseleys in action
The DO 1058 cars, of course, were not eligible to compete in the same classes as the original Minor 1000. While that was a sub-1,000cc car, the B-series engines in the Riley and Wolseley derivatives of the Minor had cubic capacities of 1,489cc, which put them into the 1,000cc-1,500cc class. (After 1962, the 1,098cc Minor 1000 was eligible for the same class, but few people were interested.)

The Riley name already had a sporting pedigree (although its major successes had been some 20 years earlier), while the Wolseley name was associated with much more staid motoring. This was the main reason why the BMC works 1½-litre cars were badged as Rileys; the other reason, of course, was that the twin-carburettor Riley had more power in standard showroom trim than the single-carburettor Wolseley. The works Rileys made their first rallying appearance in the 1958 Monte Carlo event, running unspectacularly in the Touring Car class. However, BMC also decided to use the DO 1058 design to compete in the GT class for modified cars, and to that end they prepared a very special car for works team leader John Gott. This was in a Wolseley shell (to distinguish it from the Rileys in the Touring Car class), but it was heavily modified and had a tuned MGA engine with a close-ratio gearbox. The extra performance stood Gott and his co-driver Chris Tooley in good stead and they were well up with the rally leaders when they were forced to retire after a collision with another car.

Works Rileys and works-supported Rileys ran in the 1958

Even as late as 1960, hopeful privateers were still campaigning Minors in international rallies. This 1959 948cc Minor 1000 was pictured at a checkpoint in Greoliers, on the 1960 Monte Carlo rally. Note the Town and Country tyres fitted to cope with the expected rough going.

RAC rally, and Pat Moss and Ann Wisdom switched to Rileys temporarily that year, taking the Ladies' Cup in the Circuit of Ireland event and coming second in the *Coupe des Dames* in the Tulip rally. There were Rileys in the 1959 Monte Carlo rally, too, where the Moss-Wisdom team won the *Coupe des Dames* and took fifth in their class. The 1959 RAC rally witnessed a further entry by the works' MGA-engined Wolseley, this time crewed by Douglas and Joan Johns, who took first in their class, although their overall position was 46th. Douglas Johns partnered the Rev Rupert Jones in the same car for the 1960 RAC rally, where he won the 2-litre GT class.

However, the major successes which the DO 1058 cars enjoyed were in the circuit racing which became such a feature of the British motorsports scene in the later Fifties. In 1958, the British Racing and Sports Car Club established the British Saloon Car Championship, and Rileys ran in the 1,301cc-1,600cc class against cars like the Sunbeam Rapier, the formidable Alfa-Romeo Giulietta, the PV544 and later 121 models from Volvo, and the Borgward Isabella campaigned by Bill Blydenstein.

The 1958 BSCC had One-Point-Five entries from the likes of Peter Jopp, Ian Walker, Peter Taylor and Harold Grace, but the star driver proved to be Les Leston, who went on to win his class in the 1959 championship. Leston switched to Volvo for 1960, and his place was very ably taken by Alan Hutcheson, who had first raced a One-Point-Five during 1959. During 1960, Hutcheson won 11 first places in his Riley, VUV 390, and claimed the championship in his class of the British Saloon Car Championship.

Over the next couple of years, Hutcheson's Riley continued to provide formidable competition on the tracks, and in 1961 he claimed second place overall in the BSCC. He went on to campaign his car vigorously throughout the 1963 season, but by then the writing was on the wall: the Ford Cortina GTs had arrived to dominate saloon car racing, and there was no way the 112bhp which Hutcheson had wrung out of his car was going to compete with the Lotus-developed 150bhp Cortina.

... and afterwards

Once the Minors and Rileys had retired from front-line competition, they remained popular for several years in club racing. Low cost, ready parts availability, and the ease of tuning both the A-series and B-series four-cylinder engines were the main reasons for this. Where the rules concerning modifications were more relaxed, Minors began to turn up with all sorts of engine transplants, suspension modifications and so on, until in some cases they were barely recognizable as the products of BMC's Cowley factory!

Today, Historic racing ensures that the Minors and Rileys are still actively competitive, and remain a way of enjoying some fun in saloon car racing without the need for a massive budget.

Putting more power through the back wheels of a car that was essentially a Morris Minor under the skin could sometimes make the driver busy, as this competitor discovered part-way up the famous Prescott hill-climb with his Riley One-Point-Five.

CHAPTER 9

Finding your Minor

How not to buy a rolling disaster

While I wouldn't for a minute contest the idea that the Morris Minor and its derivatives are classic cars, I would argue very strongly that they are a whole lot more than that. Many examples are still in everyday use, and I know for a fact that some of my colleagues in the teaching profession wouldn't swap their elderly Minors for a whole raft of modern Euroboxes.

So while I fully understand why many people want to own the very best and most original Minor of its type, and why they want to keep it in a heated garage in winter and only take it out to shows in the summer, my approach to Minor ownership is rather different. My main concern is whether a car is sound and usable or not. I believe that it is perfectly legitimate to update a Minor with more modern components in order to make it fit an owner's style of use more exactly, and the next chapter takes a look at what can be done in this respect. In this chapter, however, I'm concerned with the problems of finding a basically sound car in substantially unmodified condition. What you do with such a car after you've bought it is your concern, not mine.

Which Minor?

By the time you've read this far in the book, you probably already have a good idea of which Minor you'd like to own. So let me just say that the easiest models to live with are the 1,098cc models from the late Sixties, mainly because they have the best spares availability and the best road performance (though you aren't going to burn off any GTi

owners when the traffic lights go green). Convertibles are lovely cars and thoroughly practical – unless you have to park them in the street overnight, when you might wake up the next morning to find that some clown has slashed your hood. Travellers are immensely versatile, and that tends to make them a favourite for everyday use. As for the side-valve cars and the Series IIs, I'd argue that they aren't very practical for everyday use but that they are delightful machines to own if you can afford to keep one as a summer-only toy. Rileys, Wolseleys and the like? Well, you can see what I think of them in a later section.

Bodyshell and panels

If you're looking at a Minor for sale, it's pretty easy to establish whether the car is a runner or not. What is much more difficult to establish is how much structural work is going to be needed to keep it on the road for the foreseeable future. For that reason, I'm starting my advice on buying with the suggestion that you should always take a close look at the Minor's bodyshell early on in the proceedings. Convertibles, Travellers and the non-Minor relatives of the car have their own peculiarities, and so I'll deal with those later. What I'm talking about here is the saloons, both two-door and four-door.

The Minor has a monocoque bodyshell, which means that it is basically a great big metal box. Like all boxes, its strength depends on the relationship between its 'walls' and on their structural integrity: crumple one side of a cardboard box and the rest may collapse; damage one area

You may well come across a Minor in this sort of condition, but the amount of restoration needed would be far too great ever to justify the time and expense.

of a monocoque bodyshell and the rest may collapse. So the structural integrity of that monocoque is of paramount importance. What a shame that it is made of vulnerable, corrodable steel!

Nobody likes to get down on his or her hands and knees when looking at a car for sale, but I'm afraid you'll have to if you plan to check the structural integrity of a Minor. Even better, get the car onto a ramp or over a pit so that you can take a good look at the underside. You'll see that the floorpan has welded to it some reinforcing members which look much like a conventional chassis. Under the doors there are sills which extend back to support the boot area, under the front seat is a crossmember, and under the engine bay are what look like chassis rails. All of these are likely to go rusty, and when they do, they seriously weaken the car's structure.

Rusty underbody members cause other problems, too, and you can imagine what these might be just by looking at them. Rust in the rear chassis rails will threaten the security of the spring hangers, rust weakening the sills could allow the car to fold in half in a collision (or while being jacked up!), and rust in the front crossmember could weaken the torsion bar mountings and (on later cars) the jacking points. Owners have known of these danger spots for years, and a lot of Minors have been quickly and cheaply repaired in these areas to keep them on the road. Quick and cheap repairs are just that: they might last for a year or so, but they won't eradicate the problem. So beware of any patches which appear to have been welded onto the underbody members. They probably conceal rust which still needs to be cut out and will be gradually eating away at the car's structure underneath the patch panel.

Don't be content with looking underneath the car, though. Double-check by looking at the floorpan from above. To get a good look at the sills, you'll need to unscrew the kick-plates, which is well worth doing because you'd be surprised what horrors they can conceal! Lift the carpets and examine the floorpan underneath for holes and patches and – in particular – a line of rust just above the cross-member running under the front seat. Rust often starts in seams and along welds. Wet carpets or rotten underfelt demonstrate that there must have been a problem at some time, even if it has now been fixed. Find out what it was!

Next, you need to take a look at the front and rear inner wings. Rust in the rear chassis rails spreads around the rear spring hanger and up into the wheelarch, so make sure the obvious area hasn't been patched while the less visible one has been left to rot! At the front, you might well find evidence of rust at the top and bottom of the inner wing panels, and especially where the outer wing panel bolts to the inner at the top.

If all that is sound, you have found a good car. Even so, there may be rust in the panels. Front wings rust around their headlamps and (where fitted) sidelamp or indicator units, and in a characteristic vertical line just in front of the door. Rear wings suffer mostly at their bottom edges, and on two-door cars the bottom of the quarter-panel behind the door is also vulnerable. Wing panels are fairly easy to replace, fortunately, and good quality replacements can be had from specialists. Check the doors, too, for rusty bottom edges, and check the bootlid. These aren't structural areas, though, so you can put off spending money on repairs here unless the rusty panels have sharp edges which may be dangerous to pedestrians. If they do, it's an MoT failure point in Britain.

Interiors

If you look through the earlier chapters in this book, you'll see just how many different types of interior trim were fitted to the Minor over the years. Most of it is pretty hard-wearing, but you should always allow for the cost of replacing damaged items. The specialists who support the Minor can provide more or less anything nowadays, including the heat-formed trim panels of the later cars, but you shouldn't underestimate the cost of buying such items. Remember that the little tear in the driver's seat which doesn't bother you much on first sight is going to become a major annoyance after a few weeks of ownership. If the upholstery is vinyl, you will need to buy a whole replacement seat cover because vinyl can't be repaired. If the upholstery is leather, you may be able to replace just the damaged panel, but it won't be cheap to do so properly.

Engines and gearboxes

The most numerous Minors were the early 1000s with the 948cc engine. Many people will tell you that the 948cc engine is also the sweetest of the Minor types, and I wouldn't disagree with them. However, it's probably the 1,098cc Minor 1000 which survives in the greatest numbers today – partly because the cars, Travellers and LCVs with this engine are newer than the 948cc types and a greater proportion of them have been salvaged by classic-car enthusiasts.

The infamous front suspension collapse on a Minor 1000: lack of maintenance is the cause, rather than a design fault.

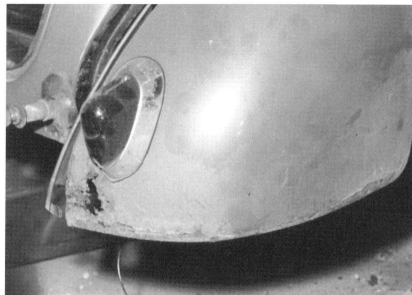

Minor rot areas (1). These pictures show rust around the wing-mounted headlamps, in the trailing edge of the front wing, in the leading edge of the rear wing, in the trailing edge of the rear wing, and along the door bottoms. All these areas can be repaired or – preferably – replaced with new panels.

Minor rot areas (2) – this time the more serious ones. These pictures show rot in the underbody near the rear spring hanger, and in the panel behind the front wheels, normally covered by the wing.

The original side-valve Minor engine gives the most lethargic performance, is the hardest to work on and the hardest to find parts for. However, if a side-valve Minor is what you want, then I wouldn't offer any words of discouragement! Frankly, though, I wouldn't recommend an 803cc Minor to anyone but the most dedicated enthusiast. The engine may be smoother than the older side-valve type, but the gearbox ratios just aren't suited to the car. Once you get into the Minor 1000s, though, the new gearbox which came in with the 948cc engine makes a really worthwhile difference.

The A-series engines have a reputation for being nigh on bullet-proof. They are simply designed and simple to maintain, and spares are readily available. If you're checking one over before purchase, look out for oil leaks from the front and rear crankshaft seals and knock the price down a bit. The leaks aren't really a major problem and can be easily fixed, but has the oil been regularly topped up or has the engine been run on very low oil? Bearing noise isn't uncommon in the A-series engines, either, although Minor enthusiasts will happily tell stories of engines which have run for tens of thousands of miles with their big-ends knocking and rumbling, so don't get too discouraged! The A-series engines are also notorious for timing-chain rattle. Once again, don't worry about it. Knock the seller's price down and make a mental note to fix it in due course; it's most unlikely that the engine will let you down.

Gearboxes are as strong as the engines, but I'd advise you to check for judder, particularly when reversing. That's most often caused by a broken strain cable between gearbox and body – a rather crude engineering solution to the problem of movement in the power train. You'll also come across a lot of cars with noisy first and reverse gears. That can be irritating, but an overhaul is one of those things you can get around to eventually rather than as a matter of urgency.

Other mechanical components

Brakes never were a strong point on the Minor, and the all-drum system is only barely adequate on the later and faster cars. Modern cars tend to stop in much shorter distances, and that encourages Minor drivers to keep a healthy space between themselves and the car in front – or to go for a disc brake conversion, as outlined in the next chapter. Handbrakes are none too efficient, either, so don't expect too much when looking over a Minor for sale.

Steering should always feel quite modern as it's a rack-and-pinion system, which was advanced for the time. If it feels sloppy, something is badly wrong. If it feels stiff, the swivel pins may be partially seized, so carry out the checks suggested below. The ride of all Minors is quite hard and can seem bouncy; don't automatically assume the dampers are at fault. Dampers in any case are consumables, but it's worth remembering that Minors have old-fashioned lever-arm dampers rather than the telescopic type used on more modern cars. These dampers last well enough and replacements can be obtained from Minor specialists. Just don't expect to be able to buy them from your local motorists' superstore: the lad behind the counter won't even know what you're talking about!

Suspension does deserve a special look when you're

Not a pretty sight! The extent of the corrosion visible here should deter all but the most dedicated enthusiast from purchasing the car – and in fact this picture was taken in a scrapyard.

checking over a car with a view to purchase, however. It isn't that the design of the suspension is poor; rather that it needs more maintenance than most owners these days are prepared to give it. The rear suspension uses cart springs and won't normally cause problems, unless leaves sag or go rusty and snap (which is rare, but can happen). It's the front suspension where the trouble lies. BMC expected owners to grease the swivel pins every 1,000 miles, which is a chore people nowadays don't expect to have to carry out. If the swivel pins aren't greased on schedule, they dry out and seize. In really bad cases, they then snap off at their top ends (where the swivel pin runs in a threaded trunnion), and the Minor's front wheel tucks itself neatly under the engine bay.

To check for problems, you need to jack up each front wheel in turn, and to look for movement at the top of the

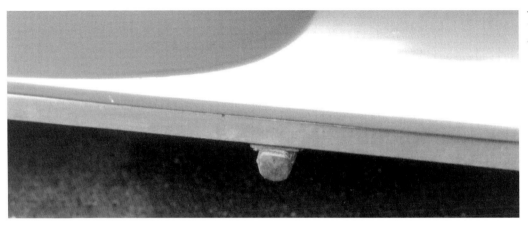

The rubber bung in the jacking point is commonly missing from Minors of all ages.

swivel pin. That movement may be a large amount of 'drop' as the weight comes off the wheel, or it may be detectable as play when the road wheel is rocked back and forth. You can also check for excess movement by getting a colleague to waggle the steering wheel back and forth as you watch what is going on under the wheelarch. Please, though, don't do this with the car supported only on a jack. Use axle stands as well; jacks have been known to collapse.

One other quirk of the Minor's suspension needs to be mentioned. If you take a car out for a road-test and attempt a full-bore standing-start, you might well discover that the result is alarming axle tramp. The bigger and more powerful the engine, the more alarming that axle tramp is likely to be. Don't let it worry you: it's quite simply a result of the relatively crude rear suspension design, and was always a problem when the cars were new. Many competition Minors were specially fitted with anti-tramp bars to counteract it, and modified Minors cope with the problem in a variety of ways, as the next chapter explains.

Convertibles

Not much needs to be said about Convertibles (and Tourers) which doesn't also apply to saloons. Their structure is basically the same as that of a two-door saloon, with a small number of reinforcing plates welded in to compensate for the absence of a fixed roof. Hoods and hood bags are the main differences. All I would suggest is that you make sure the hood mechanism works properly and hasn't seized or broken, and that the hood itself hasn't been torn. Replacements are available through the specialists – at a price.

I should also add one word of warning here. It has been possible for many years to buy well-engineered kits which will allow a two-door saloon to be turned into an authentic-looking Convertible. So not every Convertible you look at will have been built that way by the Morris factory. While there isn't anything intrinsically wrong with a converted car, many enthusiasts only want the real thing. If in doubt, check the chassis number of the car you're inspecting against the tables in Appendix B of this book.

Travellers

Travellers have some very special characteristics, and you need to be well aware of these before you start eyeing possible purchases. First of all, many Travellers were bought to work hard, and many of those for sale will have done just that. Hard work itself won't render a Traveller unfit, but the combination of hard work and zero maintenance (all too common, I'm afraid) will certainly take its toll. So don't expect the first Traveller you look at to be in pristine condition, especially if it's reasonably priced.

The next thing to remember is that the Traveller's wooden body elements are not stuck on for decoration. They really are the framework of the body structure behind the front doors. This means that any weakness in them is also a weakness in the overall structure of the car, and the MoT tester in Britain will quite rightly refuse to issue a certificate of roadworthiness to a Traveller with dodgy wood. Minor specialists can supply you with replacement wood, made to the original specifications, but it isn't cheap and it takes time and skill to rebuild a Traveller's back body properly. So take into account the cost of rebuilding a car which needs new wood if you're still tempted to buy it.

Quite often, Traveller owners will try to disguise problems with their cars' wooden body frames, either to hoodwink the MoT man or to hoodwink you – the buyer. Remember that rot often starts where two or more pieces of timber join, with the inevitable result that it attacks all of them sooner or later. You can detect rot quite easily before it gets to the seriously crumbly stage, because it shows up as dark patches on the wooden members. Some owners bleach the wood to get rid of the characteristic darkness, with the result that the treated areas look lighter than the surrounding wood. In really bad cases, owners paint the wood to disguise rot. I'd advise you not to touch a car with painted wood under any circumstances whatsoever!

LCVs

The main thing to remember about the Light Commercial Vehicle (LCV) derivatives of the Minor is that they have a separate rear chassis, which is in effect a continuation of the

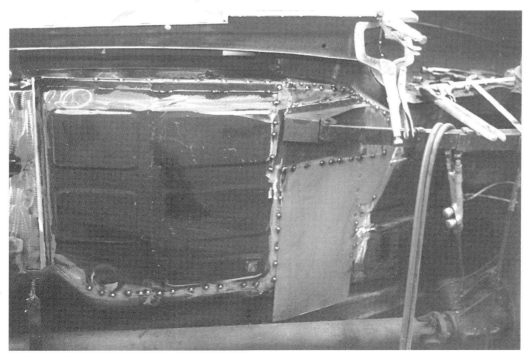

Restoration work on the underside of a Minor at Charles Ware's well-known Morris Minor Centre in Bath. Most of the panels visible here are actually new.

The Traveller's wooden body frame is subject to rot, which can be clearly seen here.

front underbody chassis rails. It rots on all four faces, and of course rust is hardest to see on the top face underneath the body. At the back of the chassis frame are brackets to which the van or pick-up body is bolted, and these brackets can rust through, so allowing the body to move about.

Bodies also have their own weaknesses. Rust quickly takes a hold in the pick-up bed, especially around the wheelarches and where the bed itself meets the bodysides. Repairs are not always straightforward. Both van and pick-up bodies rot at the junction between the wheelarches and the inner wings, and the van doors rust at their bottom edges. Body parts for these vehicles are harder to come by than body parts for their saloon equivalents. As usual, the problem is one of insufficient demand leading to difficult supply.

Rileys, Wolseleys and overseas Minors

Buying one of the non-Minor members of the Minor family needs even more care than buying a Minor. The engines and transmissions in these cars are shared with other BMC models, and the suspension and other running components are shared with the Minor itself. What this means is that mechanical spares aren't a problem. However, body and interior spares can be a headache. There are far fewer of these cars around than there are Minors, which means there is less demand for some of the items peculiar to them. That means that remanufacture isn't very attractive to specialist companies; nobody wants shelves full of slow-moving stock which cost a small fortune to make in the first place. So when buying one of these Minor derivatives, you need to be particularly choosy over the condition both of the exterior bodywork and of the interior.

Problems with the interior trim are usually fairly obvious when you start looking at a car, so I won't go into lengthy detail here. Remember, though, that there were lots of variations in colour and stitch pattern, so the chances of you finding precisely the right replacement piece of trim or upholstery in a scrap car are pretty slim. When it comes to leather trim, don't forget that although replacement and repair are possible, they are expensive.

The British-built Rileys and Wolseleys, and the Australian cars derived from them, all suffer from rusty monocoques. Look underneath first, as you would on a Minor, and check the front chassis legs, the crossmember with its torsion bar mounting points, the sills and the area around the rear spring mountings. Floors seem not to rust as badly on these cars as they do on Minors, in my experience, but it's wise to check anyway.

You'll see the same vertical line of rust at the back of the front wings as you get on Minors, and you'll probably find rust around the headlamps and in the front panel around the openings for the side grilles. A favourite rust spot is the vertical seam between the front panel and each front wing. Check for rust along the wing tops, and don't be too surprised if the wing has actually parted company with the inner valance at the top.

Have a look at the door bottoms, the rear doors around the wheelarches, the rear wheelarch itself and the bottoms of the rear wings. Unless the car you're looking at is a very well-preserved specimen, you'll certainly find rust in some of these places. It can all be cut out and remetalled, of course, but such jobs cost money unless you have the DIY skills. Don't overlook the problems with replacing chromed parts, either.

As for the mechanical components, the gearboxes are standard BMC items and are pretty tough. The Mk III type was the best of all, with stronger bearings than earlier types. The B-series engine was widely used in BMC cars and is a durable piece of machinery. It does use a certain amount of oil, and it sometimes runs on – even when in the best of health. Spares for this engine aren't generally a problem, though.

This kind of rust damage is all too common, but can easily be rectified using a replacement panel.

CHAPTER 10

The modernized Minor

Bringing it up to date

Almost from the very beginning of production, the Morris Minor has been modified to meet the varying needs of its owners. Early conversion work mostly focused on the engine, because the old side-valve four-cylinder in the original Series MM cars clearly didn't give as much performance as the 'chassis' could handle. But owners also liked to bolt on accessories of all kinds: wheel spats, external sun visors, headlamp peaks, fancy wheel trims and the like were all part of the Minor world in the Fifties and Sixties.

Things changed after the Minor went out of production in 1971. For most of the Seventies, Minors were just old cars, but the classic car movement began to show an interest in the early examples, and by the turn of the decade there was considerable enthusiasm for the Minor. The Morris Minor Owners' Club had already been founded; in 1981 Paul Skilleter wrote his ground-breaking book, *Morris Minor – The World's Supreme Small Car*, and in 1982 Charles Ware wrote an equally remarkable book called *Durable Car Ownership – A New Approach to Low-Cost Motoring*. This book showed how the planned renovation of a cheap older car like the Morris Minor could provide reliable low-cost motoring for many years.

Ware's Morris Minor Centre in Bath was a pioneer in the remanufacture of essential parts for the Minor, as well as in developing sensible specification updates to keep these cars practicable in the modern road conditions which are so very different from the conditions obtaining when they were designed.

Custom cars and hot-rods

Quite a lot of Morris Minors have also been customized (primarily for show) or hot-rodded (primarily for go). The cars remain popular in this section of the enthusiast world because they are still fairly plentiful, still fairly cheap to buy, and simply constructed (which makes modifications relatively easy). However, custom cars and hot-rods by their very nature are the result of individualistic tastes, so it isn't possible to say very much about them here except to acknowledge that they do exist.

The pictures on these pages give some idea of what can be achieved, but in reality, what can be done to a Minor is limited only by the boundaries of its owner's imagination and bank account. I should say, though, that many customized Minors incorporate some of the mechanical updates which are the main subject of this chapter.

Engines: going faster

The standard production Minor never was a fast car, which made it ideally suited to little old ladies and to teenagers learning to drive. People who want to use Minors on an everyday basis today have to face up to the fact that a car which was pretty slow in its time has been completely outclassed by humbler but more modern machinery. This is why so many of them decide to improve the Minor's performance by modifying or swapping its engine. Most updates of this sort are carried out on Minor 1000s, partly because the cars are plentiful and partly because many

Charles Ware's first 'Series III' Minor was this Traveller, which was equipped with a 1,275cc A-series engine, a Spridget gearbox, an Ital drum-braked rear axle and Ital discs on the front. The 13-inch wheels from the Ital/Marina range help to give the car a lower stance.

The 1,275cc A-series engine in Charles Ware's original Series III Traveller. This transplant has become a popular one among Minor owners.

tunable, so this simple engine swap can produce some very worthwhile performance improvements. It also has the advantage of being an engine which is actually related to the original Minor 1000 unit, a fact which appeases the conscience of many would-be purists!

Going one step further away from originality, a popular conversion centres on the Fiat Twin-Cam four-cylinder engines which were current in the Seventies and early Eighties. These engines have the twin advantages of fitting fairly easily into the Minor's engine bay and of providing quite exhilarating performance. They range in cubic capacity from 1.6 to 2.0 litres and are found in the rear-

The interior of the Ware Series III featured a number of parts taken from the Metro, including supportive seats, which were very much more comfortable than the originals for long journeys.

people feel that modifying one of the older and rarer Series IIs or MMs would be the next thing to sacrilege. I must say that I agree with them!

There isn't much doubt that the cheapest and simplest way of getting your Minor to go faster is to tune its existing engine or to swap the engine for one of the more modern variants of the A-series. The most popular choice seems to be the 1,275cc type, which delivered 65bhp in standard tune in the MG Midget and 60bhp in the Morris Marina 1.3. Those power outputs might not seem very great by modern standards, but remember that the final Minor 1000 came with just 48bhp! The 1,275cc engine is also very

Essential ingredients of the Ware Series III: the axle from a Marina or Ital, front disc brakes and struts from the same source, and front suspension arms designed to accept telescopic dampers in place of the original lever-arm type.

This modified rear suspension features anti-tramp bars and telescopic dampers.

wheel-drive 131 and 132 ranges. Best of the bunch is probably the 2-litre, which offers 112bhp in standard tune. That is more than twice as much as the original 1,098cc Minor engine, so Fiat engine transplants need to be accompanied by additional work elsewhere in the driveline, suspension and brakes.

All sorts of other engines have been dropped into Minors. I have heard (in alphabetical order) of cars with engines made by Datsun (the A-series four-cylinders), Ford (Cortina four-cylinder and V4), Holden (six-cylinder), Isuzu, Mazda (both in-line four-cylinder and rotary twin), Peugeot, Rover (the V8), Simca (the Vedette V8), Toyota (both eight-valve and 16-valve four-cylinders), Vauxhall/Opel (the Astra 16-valve) and Volkswagen (Golf). Even the old BMC B-series four-cylinder, in various capacities from 1.5 to 1.8 litres, has also found its way into Minors.

Obviously, some of these transplants are more difficult than others, and any engine which was originally installed transversely is going to be rather harder to adapt to the Minor's north-south mountings. You need to take plenty of professional advice before embarking on a transplant, and ideally to go and look at a few cars which have already been fitted with the engine you have in mind. Don't decide that you'll use a particular engine just because you can get one cheaply, because you might find the extra expense of the installation eating away at the savings you thought you'd made.

Gearboxes: all-synchro and five speeds

The gearbox in the Minor 1000 is quite a nice little unit, but it doesn't have synchromesh on first gear like a modern gearbox. If you want to go for an all-synchromesh gearbox, the Morris Marina item is an obvious choice, especially if you're fitting the Marina 1,275cc engine as well. However, it isn't as easy to fit as you might expect, and a fair amount of work is involved.

The other shortcoming of the Minor's gearbox, at least by modern standards, is that it has only four speeds. Drivers of modern cars are used to five-speed gearboxes with the fifth

A telescopic damper in place on the front wishbone assembly. Note the disc brake and the pick-up point for the anti-roll bar ...

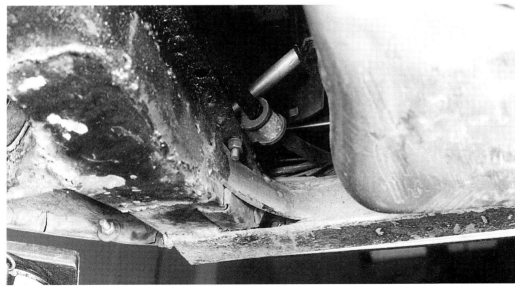

... which can be seen again here.

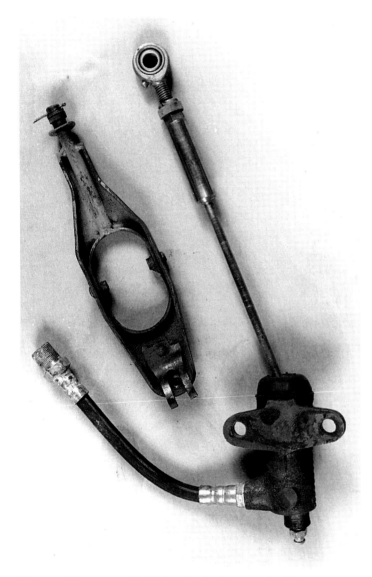

The constituent parts of a hydraulic clutch conversion kit.

speed being an overdrive for motorway cruising, and if you do a lot of motorway work in your Minor, you'll certainly appreciate the more relaxed high-speed cruising which an overdrive top gear can bring.

There are two ways of achieving this. One way is to fit an overdrive unit to the back of the existing gearbox. The one to use was fitted to various Triumphs during the Seventies – the Spitfire Mk IV, Spitfire 1500 and Dolomite – and is well supported by Triumph specialists. Proper conversions have been developed by Minor specialists, and you should always be prepared to pay for the benefit of their experience and advice. The overdrive is, of course, switched in and out electrically.

The second method of achieving more relaxed motorway cruising is to fit a modern five-speed gearbox. One popular choice is a Toyota unit which was fitted to the Celica in the Eighties, but if you are going for an engine transplant as well it is probably worth finding out whether your chosen engine was available with a five-speed gearbox and, if so, whether that gearbox can be fitted into a Minor. It is much easier to transplant engine and gearbox as a unit than to try to match an engine from one manufacturer to the gearbox from another, especially when the host car is from yet a third! In most cases, fitting a non-standard gearbox will involve bellhousing changes, juggling with clutch components, making up a special crossmember to support the gearbox, and shortening the propshaft. You might also have trouble finding a speedometer cable of the correct length.

In theory, there is no reason why you shouldn't fit your Minor with an automatic transmission if you want to. I've never come across one yet, but I have heard stories about such conversions. The only advice I'd give is that most automatics are best with larger-capacity engines, especially in a fairly heavy car like the Minor.

Front suspension
The Minor's torsion-bar front suspension was very advanced in 1948 and wore well. However, it was matched to lever-arm dampers (which can only be bought from specialist outlets now), and more modern suspension

This fabricated crossmember supports the rear of a non-standard gearbox.

Well organized ... the component parts of the transplant kit made by Unique Autocraft which allows a Fiat Twin-Cam engine to be fitted quite easily into a Morris Minor. Power outputs up to 112bhp in untuned form are then available.

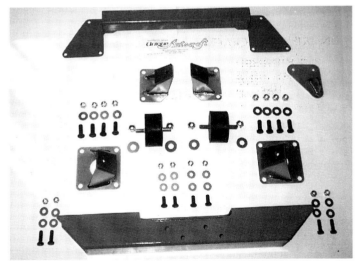

technology has also brought the possibility of better handling. Fitting modern low-profile tyres on wider rims in conjunction with improved suspension (both front and rear) is an accepted way of improving a Minor these days. It puts more rubber on the road for better roadholding and safer stopping and, of course, replacement modern low-profile radial tyres are far easier to find, and often cheaper, than the original crossplies fitted to the Minor.

It certainly is worth switching to telescopic dampers at the front end, perhaps in combination with other modifications such as disc brakes and wider wheels. The telescopic dampers help to prevent nose-dive under heavy braking, and tend to make the front end more stable. In addition, replacements are both easy to find and cheaper than replacement lever-arm dampers. Proper conversion kits can be bought through Minor specialists, and are relatively simple to fit and not particularly expensive for the benefits they bring.

Source of inspiration? The Morris Marina was supposed to replace the Minor in British Leyland's range, but it never caught the public imagination in the same way. However, today, the cars have a value as a useful source of parts for modernizing the Minor ...

Rear suspension

There are two problems with the Minor's simple rear suspension. The first is that it gives a rather skittish ride over poor surfaces, which doesn't inspire confidence in the driver and is also likely to provoke rear-seat passengers into asking him or her to slow down. The second is that a heavy application of power from a standing start tends to result in axle tramp, as the poorly-located axle bounces uncontrollably up and down before the tyres bite and the car gets under way. Axle tramp is always at its worst in a tuned Minor.

The simplest way of coping with this is to fit not only telescopic dampers but also anti-tramp bars. You can get both from the acknowledged Minor specialists, who have plenty of experience of fitting such components and can supply conversion kits. More radical solutions are not uncommon, and many owners have fitted complete rear axles from the Morris Marina, Toyota Celica Mk I, Ford Escort or Ford Capri. These axles are also stronger than the standard Minor item, and are therefore one good way of dealing with the extra stresses put on the half-shafts and differential by an engine which is significantly more powerful than the original.

Brakes

The Minor's brakes were never one of its better features, and a simple way of improving stopping power is to fit the larger drums from a Riley One-Point-Five or Wolseley 1500 – if you can find some. More radical, but ultimately much more satisfying – not to mention comforting – is to fit disc brakes to the front wheels.

There are two favourite sources of disc brakes for the Minor, and specialists can supply the parts for the conversion and the expertise for their installation. One source is the MG Midget (or Austin-Healey Sprite), and the level of enthusiasm for these cars means that the

The Minor has been a favourite on the custom car scene for many years. This much-modified 1967 pick-up is known as 'Black Overdose', and features height-adjustable suspension. It was photographed by Tony Aston for *Minor Monthly* magazine

This customized Minor started life as a GPO van! Robin Beardmore turned it into a pick-up with detachable cab panels, fitting disc brakes, a 2-litre Fiat Twin-Cam engine, a five-speed Fiat gearbox and the rear axle from a Toyota Celica. It was photographed for *Minor Monthly* magazine by Robert Hawkins.

Somebody had to do it, and the Oakdale Morris Minor Centre in Manchester were the ones who did. Fans of Enid Blyton's Noddy will have no difficulty in recognizing the source of inspiration for this customized Minor, pictured by Tony Aston for *Minor Monthly* magazine.

Sensible and discreet modifications include fitting a brake servo (bottom left) and replacing the dynamo with an alternator (right).

support industry which provides parts for them is going to be around for many years to come. The second source is the Morris Marina, which has slightly larger discs but different hubs, so that you will need modified hubs if you wish to retain the Minor's original wheels. Many owners like to fit the 13-inch Marina wheels instead of the Minor's original 14-inch variety, though, and you can get an idea of the pros and cons of each option by talking to the Minor specialists.

It's worth knowing that the standard Minor brake master cylinder is too small to cope with the extra fluid needed for disc brakes to function correctly. You can either fit an auxiliary reservoir or a different master cylinder (which isn't a bad idea in view of the inaccessibility of the original!). Many people think that it's worth fitting a servo with disc brakes, and a good installation will certainly give plenty of reassuring stopping power.

Overall
What I certainly wouldn't recommend is a 'piecemeal' upgrading of a Minor. You need to decide what you're trying to achieve and plan it carefully, making sure that you treat the exercise as an upgrade of the whole car and not just an upgrade of part of it. It's obvious that a more powerful engine ought to be matched by more powerful brakes, and that any significant increase in road performance is best matched by improvements in the handling and roadholding as well.

Don't think only of the mechanical side, either: if you insist on taking your newly revitalized Minor around corners on its door-handles, you'll soon find that the standard seats are pretty unsupportive. Think about fitting more modern seats with better lateral support and even headrests – those from a Metro are ideal, and the specialists will even re-upholster them to match your existing interior.

If modifying a Minor appeals to you, I wish you the very best of luck. You'll end up with a reliable and distinctive means of transport which will last you for many years and won't have cost as much as the humblest of brand-new Euroboxes. That, surely, is what Alec Issigonis would have wanted for the Minor's long-term future.

APPENDIX A

Technical specifications

Morris Minor Series MM models, 1948-1953

Engine: Side-valve four-cylinder, type USHM2. 57mm bore x 90mm stroke, giving 918cc. Single SU type H1 1⅛in carburettor and 6.5:1 or 6.7:1 compression ratio. Power output 27bhp at 4,400rpm; maximum torque 39 lb.ft at 2,400rpm (high compression engine).

Transmission: Four-speed gearbox with synchromesh on 2nd, 3rd and 4th gears only. Gear ratios 3.95:1. 2.30:1, 1.54:1, 1.00:1, reverse 3.95:1. Axle ratio 4.22:1.

Steering, suspension and brakes: Independent front suspension with wishbones and torsion bar springs. Live rear axle with semi-elliptic leaf springs. Armstrong lever-arm hydraulic dampers on all four wheels. Rack-and-pinion steering. Drum brakes all round. 14-inch wheels with 5.00 x 14 tyres.

Dimensions: Wheelbase 86in. Front track 50.6in. Rear track 50.3in. Length 148in. Width 61in. Height 60in. Unladen weight 1,735 lb approx (two-door saloon).

Derivatives: Two-door saloon and Tourer (1948-1953); four-door saloon (1950-1953).

Morris Minor Series II models, 1952-1956

All details as for Series MM models, except:

Engine: Overhead-valve four-cylinder, type APHM. 58mm bore x 76.2mm stroke, giving 803cc. Single SU type H1 1⅛in carburettor and 7.2:1 compression ratio. Power output 30bhp at 4,800rpm; maximum torque 40 lb.ft at 2,400rpm.

Transmission: Gear ratios 4.09:1, 2.588:1, 1.679:1, 1.00:1, reverse 5.174:1. Axle ratio 4.55:1 to the end of 1953, 5.375:1 thereafter and on all Travellers.

Derivatives: Two-door saloon, Tourer and four-door saloon available throughout the production run; Traveller, van and pick-up all available from 1953.

Morris Minor 1000 (948cc) models, 1956-1962

All details as for Series II models, except:

Engine: Overhead-valve four-cylinder, type APJM or 9M. 62.9mm bore x 76.2mm stroke, giving 948cc. Single SU type H2 1¼in carburettor (1956-1960) or type HS2 1¼in carburettor (from 1960) and 8.3:1 or 7.2:1 compression ratio. Power output 37bhp at 4,750rpm; maximum torque 48 lb.ft at 3,000rpm (high compression engine).

Transmission: Gear ratios 3.628:1, 2.374:1, 1.412:1, 1.000:1, reverse 4.664:1.

Derivatives: Two-door saloon and Tourer, four-door saloon, Traveller, van and pick-up.

Morris Minor 1000 (1,098cc) models, 1962-1971

All details as for earlier Minor 1000 models, except:

Engine: Overhead-valve four-cylinder, type 10MA. 64.5mm bore x 83.7mm stroke, giving 1,098cc. Single SU type HS2 1¼in carburettor and 8.5:1 or 7.5:1 compression ratio. Power output 48bhp at 5,100rpm; maximum torque 60 lb.ft at 2,500rpm (high compression engine).

Steering, suspension and brakes: 5.20 x 14 tyres; radial 145 x 14 size optional from 1968.

Derivatives: Two-door and four-door saloons (to 1970), Tourer (to 1969), Traveller, van and pick-up (to 1971).

Riley One-Point-Five models, 1957-1965

Engine: Overhead-valve four-cylinder, B-series. 73.02mm bore x 88.9mm stroke, giving 1,489cc. Two SU type H4 1¼in carburettors and 8.3:1 compression ratio. Power output 68bhp at 5,400rpm; maximum torque 83 lb.ft at 3,000rpm.

Transmission: Four-speed gearbox with synchromesh on 2nd, 3rd and 4th gears only. Gear ratios 3.635:1, 2.212:1, 1.373:1, 1.000:1, reverse 4.753:1. Axle ratio 3.73:1.

Steering, suspension and brakes: Independent front suspension with wishbones and torsion bar springs. Live rear axle with semi-elliptic leaf springs. Armstrong lever-arm hydraulic dampers on all four wheels. Rack-and-pinion steering. Drum brakes all round. 14-inch wheels with 5.00 x 14 tyres.
Dimensions: Wheelbase 86in. Front track 50.6in. Rear track 50.3in. Length 153in. Width 61in. Height 60in (Mk III models 57in). Unladen weight 2,104 lb approx.
Derivatives: Four-door saloon.

Wolseley 1500 models, 1957-1965
Engine: Overhead-valve four-cylinder, B-series. 73.02mm bore x 88.9mm stroke, giving 1,489cc. SU type H2 1¼in carburettor and 7.2:1 compression ratio. Power output 50bhp at 4,200rpm; maximum torque 74 lb.ft at 3,000rpm.
Transmission: Four-speed gearbox with synchromesh on 2nd, 3rd and 4th gears only. Gear ratios and axle ratio as for Riley One-Point-Five.
Steering, suspension and brakes: Independent front suspension with wishbones and torsion bar springs. Live rear axle with semi-elliptic leaf springs. Armstrong lever-arm hydraulic dampers on all four wheels. Rack-and-pinion steering. Drum brakes all round. 14-inch wheels with 5.00 x 14 tyres.
Dimensions: Wheelbase 86in. Front track 50.6in. Rear track 50.3in. Length 152in. Width 61in. Height 60in (Mk III models 57in). Unladen weight 2,060 lb approx.
Derivatives: Four-door saloon.

Austin Lancer Series I models, 1958-1959
Engine: Overhead-valve four-cylinder, B-series. 73.02mm bore x 88.9mm stroke, giving 1,489cc. Single carburettor.
Transmission: Four-speed gearbox with synchromesh on 2nd, 3rd and 4th gears only.
Steering, suspension and brakes: Independent front suspension with wishbones and torsion bar springs. Live rear axle with semi-elliptic leaf springs. Lever-arm hydraulic dampers on all four wheels. Rack-and-pinion steering. Drum brakes all round. 14-inch wheels with 5.00 x 14 tyres.
Dimensions: Wheelbase 86in. Front track 50.6in. Rear track 50.3in. Length 152in. Width 61in. Height 60in.
Derivatives: Four-door saloon.

Austin Lancer Series II models, 1959-1962
All details as for Austin Lancer Series I, except:
Dimensions: Wheelbase 92in.

Morris Major Series I models, 1958-1959
All details as for Austin Lancer Series I models.

Morris Major Series II models, 1959-1962
All details as for Austin Lancer Series II models.

Morris Major Elite models, 1962-1964
All details as for Morris Major Series II models, except:
Engine: Overhead-valve four-cylinder, B-series. 76.2mm bore x 88.9mm stroke, giving 1,622cc. Single carburettor.

Car number sequences and production figures

A. Number sequences for cars

Series MM Minor, September 1948 to March 1952

All cars had numbers prefixed with SMM, followed by a serial number in the range 501 to 13948. The car number plate on the engine side of the bulkhead also carried an additional type code, as follows:

MNR   Cellulose paint

MNR/S   Synobel paint

MNR/SYN   Synthetic paint

(The code MNR was the Nuffield code for the Minor range.)

Series II Minor, April 1952 to February 1953
Minor 1000, March 1953 to mid-1958

Until January 1958, car numbers had 11 digits, consisting of five identifying code letters and a six-digit serial number. From January 1958, the fifth code letter (indicating paint type) was omitted to give 10-digit numbers.

Make and model	Body type	Colour
F = Morris Minor	A = four-door	A = Black
	B = two-door	B = Grey
	C = Tourer	C = Red
	L = Traveller	D = Blue
		E = Green

Specification	Paint type	Serial number
1 = RHD, home	1 = synthetic	139439 to 666000
2 = RHD, export	2 = Synobel *	
3 = LHD, export	3 = cellulose *	
4 = North America, export		
5 = RHD, CKD		
6 = LHD, CKD		

* in practice, synthetic paint was standard on Series II cars

Minor 1000 (948cc), from mid-1958
Minor 1000 (1,098cc)

The third-generation Minors had 10-digit, 11-digit or 12-digit car numbers, consisting of a four-digit identifying prefix followed by a six-digit or seven-digit serial number, plus a final suffix letter on some cars. The identifying prefix letters decode as follows: M = Morris, A = A-series engine, S = saloon, T = Tourer, W = Traveller. Some late 1,098cc models also carry a second suffix letter to indicate the build location, the choices being M for Cowley and F for Adderley Park. (In practice, all saloons were built at Cowley.)

Identifying prefix (1)	Identifying prefix (2)
MA = Morris, A-series engine	S3 = four-door saloon, Series 3
	2S = two-door saloon
	T3 = Tourer, Series 3
	W3 = Traveller, Series 3

Serial number	Suffix letter (when present)
666001 to 1294082	D = De Luxe model (not always present)
	L = Left-hand-drive

Riley One-Point-Five

The first 150 Rileys, built at Abingdon, had five-digit car numbers, consisting of a two-digit identifying code and a three-digit serial number. The remaining cars had seven-digit, eight-digit or nine-digit car numbers, consisting of a four-digit identifying prefix followed by a three-, four- or five-digit serial number.

Abingdon-built Mk I models, 1957

Identifying code
VA = Riley One-Point-Five

Serial number
501 to 650

Mk I and Mk II models, 1957-1961

Identifying code (1)	Identifying code (2)	Identifying code (3)
HS = DO 1058 type	R = Riley	1 = first version

Serial number
260 to 27897

Mk III models, 1961-1965

Identifying code (1)	Identifying code (2)	Identifying code (3)
R = Riley	HS = DO 1058 type	2 = second version

Serial number
101 to 12184

Wolseley 1500

The Wolseleys had seven-digit, eight-digit or nine-digit car numbers, consisting of a four-digit identifying prefix followed by a three-, four- or five-digit serial number.

Mk I models, 1957-1959

Identifying code (1)	Identifying code (2)	Identifying code (3)
W = Wolseley	A1 = DO 1058 type	L = low-compression engine
		Second 'L' (eg WA1LL 1234) indicates LHD

Serial number
101 to 32400

Mk I and Mk II models, 1959-1961

Identifying code (1)	Identifying code (2)	Identifying code (3)
W = Wolseley	WA = DO 1058 type	1 = first version

Serial number
32401 to 69054

Mk III models, 1961-1965

Identifying code (1)	Identifying code (2)	Identifying code (3)
W = Wolseley	HS = DO 1058 type	2 = second version

Serial number
101 to 32096

B. Number sequences for Light Commercials

Series II, 803cc, May 1953 to September 1956
Series III, 948cc, September 1956 to January 1962 approx.
Until January 1958, car numbers had eight, nine , 10 or 11 digits, consisting of five identifying code letters or numbers and a three- four-, five- or six-digit serial number. From January 1958, the fifth digit of the code (indicating paint type) was omitted to give 10-digit numbers.

Make and model	Body type	Colour
O = Morris Minor commercial	E = van	B = Light Grey
	F = pick-up	C = Dark Red (GPO mail vans)
	G = chassis/cab	D = Dark Blue
	H = GPO mail van	E = Green
	I = GPO engineers' van	F = Beige
	K = bare chassis	H = Primer or CKD finish

Specification	Paint type	Serial number
1 = RHD, home	1 = synthetic	501 to 149536 approx.
2 = RHD, export	5 = primer only	
3 = LHD, export		
4 = North America, export		
5 = RHD, CKD		
6 = LHD, CKD		

Series III, 948cc, January to September 1962
Series V, 1,098cc, September 1962 to December 1971
These Light Commercials had 10-digit, 11-digit or 12-digit car numbers, consisting of a four-digit identifying prefix followed by a six-digit or seven-digit serial number, plus a final suffix letter on some vehicles. Some late 1,098cc models also carry a further suffix letter to indicate the build location, the choices being M for Cowley and F for Adderley Park.

Identifying prefix (1)
MA = Morris, A-series engine

Identifying prefix (2)
E5 = Telephone engineers' van, Series V
G5 = GPO mail van, Series V
Q5 = chassis/cab, Series V
U5 = pick-up, Series V
V5 = van, Series V

Serial number
137654 approx to 327369

Suffix letter (when present)
L = Left-hand-drive

Austin-badged variants,
February 1968 approx to December 1971
These Light Commercials had 10-digit car numbers, consisting of a four-digit identifying prefix followed by a six-digit serial number.

Identifying prefix (1)
AA = Austin, A-series engine

Identifying prefix (2)
QC = chassis/cab
UC = pick-up
VC = van

Serial number
236504 to 327369

C. Production totals for Morris Minor and Light Commercials

It is unfortunately not possible to break the production figures down into individual model variants, as surviving records group all car variants – two-door and four-door saloons, Tourers and Travellers – into the same sequence.

Series MM

1948 1,215		**1951** 48,341	
1949 28,590		**1952** 45,870	
1950 48,061		**1953** 3,925	

Total 176,002

Series II

1952 1,947		**1955** 88,773	
1953 55,176		**1956** 68,916	
1954 73,491			

Total 288,303

Minor 1000 (948cc)   *(NB: All figures are approximate)*

1957 103,944		**1960** 95,350	
1958 115,000		**1961** 60,800	
1959 107,000		**1962** 58,385	

Total 540,479

Minor 1000 (1,098cc)

1963 45,900	**1968** 31,640*
1964 41,385	**1969** 28,275*
1965 39,008	**1970** 20,102
1966 38,610	**1971** 5,705
1967 37,922	
	Total 288,547

* Approximate figures only

Overall production totals for the Minor and its Light Commercial derivatives are still the subject of some debate. The figures given below come from a different source, and it will be obvious from the figures in the last column where there are discrepancies.

Model	Cars	Light Commercials	Total
Series MM	176,002		176,002
Series II	269,838	48,513	318,351
Minor 1000 (948cc)	544,048	100,631	644,679
Minor 1000 (1,098cc)	303,443	177,482	480,825
	1,293,331	**326,626**	**1,619,857**

D. Production totals for Riley and Wolseley saloons

Riley One-Point-Five

Mk I	Mk II	Mk III	Total
17,621	9,776	12,084	39,481

Wolseley 1500

Mk I	Mk II	Mk III	Total
46,438	22,295	31,989	100,722

How fast? How economical? How heavy?
Performance figures for classic Minors

	Series MM Tourer	Series MM 4-door	Series II 4-door	1000 De Luxe 4-door 948cc	1000 De Luxe 4-door 1,098cc	Riley One-point-Five
Max speed (mph)	60	61	64.7	74.4	73.4	80.2
Acceleration (sec)						
0-30mph	8.7	9.8	8.4	6.9	6.6	5.2
0-40mph	15.9	-	14.9	12.3	9.9	8.2
0-50mph	29.2	38.5	28.6	18.7	16.1	12.5
0-60mph	-	-	-	30.1	24.8	18.9
Standing ¼-mile (sec)	27.1	-	26.5	24.1	22.8	20.9
Acceleration in top gear (sec)						
10-30mph	18.2	23.5	15.9	14.2	-	11.8
20-40mph	21.3	23.4	17.6	14.9	13.6	13.1
30-50mph	28.6	36.8	24.1	17.1	16.3	14.8
Overall fuel consump'n (mpg)	42	35-40	39.3	36.3	31.2	25.7
Weight	14.5 cwt (unladen)	16cwt (on test)	15.75cwt (unladen)	15.5cwt (kerb)	15.25cwt (kerb)	18.5cwt (kerb)
Original test published	*Motor* Aug 23, 1950	*Autocar* May 4, 1951	*Motor* Jan 28, 1953	*Motor* Nov 22, 1956	*Autocar* May 8, 1964	*Motor* Jan 11, 1961